Spillway

Spillway

volume 3, issue 1

guest edited by
Douglas Manuel & Steven Reigns

MOON
TIDE PRESS

~ 2025 ~

Spillway: volume 3, issue 1
© Copyright 2025 Moon Tide Press

Editor-in-chief
Eric Morago

***Spillway* Associate Editors**
Alyssa Murray
Shelly Holder
Ellen Webre

Guest Editors
Douglas Manuel & Steven Reigns

Front cover art
"An Open Book" by Nancy Beagle

Book design
Michael Wada

Moon Tide logo design
Abraham Gomez

Spillway logo design
Amanda Le

Spillway: volume 3, issue 1
is published by Moon Tide Press

Moon Tide Press
6709 Washington Ave. #9297
Whittier, CA 90608
www.moontidepress.com

FIRST EDITION

Printed in the United States of America

ISBN # 978-1-957799-38-4

Table of Contents

Foreword by Alyssa Murray   *12*

00: BORN TO DIE AGAIN

Marie Scarles
  A Spell for Living   16

Emily Tallman
  The Most Ordinary Thing   17

Jane Zich
  Alone In the Studio   18

01: MOTHER!

Susan Niz
  Pelagic   20

Alicia Vogl Saenz
  Quito, February 1928   21
  Urban Parrots   22

02: RELENTLESS LIFE

Elaine Mintzer
  Botanic Garden Built Over a Landfill   24

Amy Small-McKinney & Dick Westheimer
  We Are What We Listen For   25

Hilda Weiss
  Like the Parrots   26

Aruni Wijesinghe
    Disco Jesus   27
    Revive   29

03: DYING ALIVE

Nancy Beagle
    Eyes on Music   32
    Reinvention   33

Nathaniel Dolton-Thornton
    aether/oar   34

Lesley Rogers Hobbs
    ~~House For Sale:~~ SOLD   37

Rachel Neve Midbar
    The Demon You Read   38

Chanel Brenner
    Let's Keep the Cat   39
    Exit Way   41

Rachel Walker
    Half-Ghost   43

Aleksandra Scepanovic
    Lost   44
    The Vanishing   45

Michael J. Galko
    A week in Japan as a smoker   46

Gahl Liberzon
    Post-Mortum   48

Todd Robinson
    I See Her from the Spare Bedroom   50

04: INOPERABLE

Ron Koertge
ICU   52
The Prophet Isaiah   53

Therese Gleason
In the Negative   54

Nancy Beagle
Let the Fish Go?   56

Patricia Davis-Muffett
What It's Like to Be Human   58

Patricia L. Scruggs
Bones, Them Cracked Bones   59

Peggy Dobreer
Car Sick   61

Amanda Le
That Which Was Forgotten   62
Postmortem   63

Alexis Rhone Fancher
The God for Broken People   64

05: BLIND AWAKENING

Yvette R. Murray
After Hearing the Truth, Woman Walks Alone in the Fog 66

Robbi Nester
Legacy   67
Golden Shovel, from a line by Emily Dickinson   68

Brian Sonia-Wallace
    Grace   69
    Instructions for Living   70

Terri Niccum
    Relinquished   71

Ben Trigg
    Inferno   73

Jane Zich
    Spirit of Renewal   74
    Revision   75

06: GROWING PAINS

Charles Harper Webb
    Dissection Day   78

Alexis Rhone Fancher
    Walking on Water   80
    I'm Not Poisonous, I'm Just Drawn that Way   81

Michael Juliani
    Amazing Grace, Imagine, Hallelujah   82

Patricia Behrens
    Saul Bernstein   84

Susan Hayden
    I Didn't Know How to Twist   85

J.D. Isip
    Homing   89
    The Myth of the Magikarp   90

Edward Garza
    Andre in the Cave   91

07: UTTERANCE

Mariano Zaro
    The Mercy of Memory   94

Lao Rubert
    Words Are Not   96

Shirley J. Brewer
    Poem Beginning with a Line from Richard Hugo   97

Joanne Clarkson
    Daring the Re-Discovered Life   98

Trish Holden
    On the Way   99

Brian Duran-Fuentes
    The Returned   100

LeAnne Hunt
    Idaho   101
    The god of lint   102

08: OVERRIPE

Kami Nzeribe
    She Is Everywhere   103
    Taste it. She is Everywhere!   104

Stephanie Barbé Hammer
    The Tired Magician   106

Kim Dower
    Why It's Important to Kill Ants   111
    How to Celebrate the End of the World   112

Rob Kunz
    A Soul's Descent Two Ways   113

09: REUNITE

Janet McMillan Rives
    Grafted   116

Kareem Tayyar
    The Queen of Snow   117

Robb Kunz
    Color Story First Band   127
    As Far as Pieces Missing   128
    Gaia in Tree Form   129
    Into Black and White   130
    Leafless   131

Nancy Issenman
    Reincarnation: Notes to Self   132

Diane Douiyssi
    to soar   134

About the Contributors   136
About the Guest Editors   149
Notes and Acknowledgments   150

Foreword

I've always had trouble grasping the purpose of literary magazines. Thirty, fifty, one hundred-ish pages of struggling artists' best feet forward sounds idyllic at best and futile at worst. After all, the people most likely to read contemporary works are likely too busy producing their own to actually have the time to do so. Between the lack of readership, overly competitive submissions, and staggering potential for pretentious pseudo-literature, it's easy enough to think of lit mags as nothing more than a nicely-formatted waste of trees.

It wasn't until I was invited to be an associate editor for *Spillway* that I stopped being a traitor to my own kind of small-time writers and realized the capacity for personal expression that literary magazines have for writers and readers alike as the modern embodiment of "Art for Art's Sake." I've written and edited books, essays, and countless poems, but compiling and arranging Volume 3, Issue 1 of *Spillway* may have been the most influential work I've done thus far in my literary career. By prioritizing creative expression as a value to ground the magazine, my work on this issue of *Spillway* made me realize that, for all their flaws, literary magazines provide a unique conduit for approaching literature the way we did before the days of Big 5 publishers: artistically.

The theme of this issue is *Rebirth*, and my goal in editing this edition was to make the content's arrangement as equally thematic as the pieces themselves. Rather than the classic alphabetical order many literary magazines put their pieces in, this issue of *Spillway* creates a chronology of life, death, and rebirth to emphasizes the cyclic nature between them. We begin with the beginning of a terrestrial existence marked by suffering; then, death extinguishes this existence; and, finally, another chance at life emerges through the ethereum. Physical death acts as a conduit for mental transcendence, but the physical must be reconciled with the psychical for both of them to reach their peaks. The spirit, the *res cognitas,* the "thinking thing" in all of us can only find its purpose as it relates to the body. We are only agents in the physical world so much as we are physical beings, yet earthly suffering drives a wedge between mental and material states. This disconnect thus necessitates a rejoinment; a reconciliation; a *rebirth.*

Rebirth is multipathed and equifinal. In the metaphysical sense, it may look like complete philosophical or moral upheaval; In the spiritual, turning to God, reincarnation, anything that permits one to be born again through a vital trust in the universe; In the physical, perhaps, going on a juice cleanse and trading in our morning donuts for a brisk jog. The only 'wrong' way to be reborn is to crawl back into the womb–to retreat into spaces that no longer fit our grown, battered bodies. Rebirth is within and beyond us, but inextricably *ours*.

There being no one way to go about rebirth brings me back to literary magazines as an expressive form. *Spillway*'s history in the poetry community has touched every corner of poetics: the weird, the raw, the thoughts that probably shouldn't have made it to the page in the first place. By incorporating this multitude of forms and their unique authors in our publication, we embody the spirit of rebirth as an individual process of discovery.

As you read through this issue of *Spillway*, you will bear witness to a single narrative of creation, life, and transcendence told through parallel forward motion. Like beads on a string, these works are each unique, but work together to tell the same story. This story is timeless and foretold, trite as all hell but truer for it–it is the story of the human experience as we outgrow coincidence and step into intentionality. Agency, independence, individuality: whatever you want to call it, it is unapologetic, it is there, and it is at our fingertips, waiting for us to rip it open and make it our own. (Much like the copy of *Spillway* in your hand!)

Poetry is the connective tissue between the imaginative and material world that allows us to be reborn. Though I can't promise you'll be reincarnated after skimming this issue, I hope the poems and the collective story they tell will empower you to track their cyclic narrative of living and dying, those markers that punctuate our experiences to make us feel whole, unique, and greater than the sum of our parts…or, to put it more simply, *born again.*

Alyssa Murray
Associate Editor, *Moon Tide Press*

REBIRTH
00: BORN TO DIE AGAIN

Marie Scarles

A Spell for Living

I was born
with the heart of an artist
and the mind of a starfish. I was born
with the bones of a whale and an eye
on the sea. You were born with me

and we met there in the water,
as we rose to meet the ocean's
topmost coat. We reveled in it,
the planet spinning on tiny toes.

Back then, we were cute as babies
eating cake for the first time ever, eyes
large as saucers. We were clams, or happy as,
under the trillion-fracture face
of the sea. Mortality rises
like a threatened snake.
Let it leave my tall body behind.

Emily Tallman

The Most Ordinary Thing

I was eating cherries on the porch that morning as
my mom died, chewing the meat from smooth white
seeds and spitting them into the dirt. Chewing and
spitting and chewing and spitting, a rite to hold the
fast dissolving day, when far below a pit unfurled
her roots and pushed a shoot up. Beyond the porch,
the shoot became a tree, her wide leaves trembling
with a phantom breath, and there was no second
glance from the hawk in the cloud, or the neighbor
taking out the trash, when her branches bore fruit
and the fruit ripened, the seeds falling back into the
dirt, from which another tree grew and bore fruit,
and another, and then another, each one withering
back into the earth as the next one came to life,
entire generations passing before me like the most
ordinary thing in the world.

Jane Zich

Alone In the Studio

01: MOTHER!

Pelagic

My notebook is my biological mother.
She accepts my handwritten confession

I'd like to write a geologic line
About how I spiraled into this

From pre-historical fear
My two feet: littoral, never pelagic.

From the edge, never immersed in
The salty depths. As I dream, what swims?

I want to spew from deep sea volcanoes
Instead, my soul: beached jellyfish, sandpiper

I didn't know how to keep the water
From entering my nose.

List fear in my biographical statement
No one set me straight (the notebook only listens)

No one tells you beauty is unconditional.

I'll step off the edge of this before the snow melts
Before I know the names of Mariana-trench minerals.

Alicia Vogl Saenz

Quito, February 1928

Quito is built high in the Andes on the foundation of a destroyed
Incan city, cradled in the foothills of an active volcano. Altitude thin
air squeezes lungs. Streets are cobblestone and narrow, houses have
thick adobe walls, whitewashed, and feel like stone. Courtyards and
big trees. Omniscient sun at noon, rain every afternoon falls like
whispers. Fog folds in at dusk. Dampness permeates. Buried deep
underground lies the knowledge that the volcano could erupt at any
moment. The fog, the thin air, and the massive Andean landscape
feel like being shut in. Quito is like Jane's England and Federico's
Spain: a ruined girl ruins a family. Abuelita is nineteen years old. Of
course, she is not Abuelita yet. She is a girl who lives with her mother
and brothers who study medicine or law. Servants stir and chop, fold
and dust, wash and scrub. Abuelita crochets.

I can't know any of this, really. My sister and I wonder about the
how of our mami's conception. My sister says she heard there was a
military school across the street. We know he was an officer. I heard
that he was invited to stay in the house. We know he was married.
The Abuelita we know is not a coqueta. Body carried stiffly; blouse
buttoned. Una mujer seria who crocheted by the light of the TV's
blue glow. Did he show up in her bedroom? *I just needed to see you.
You smiled at me across the table at lunch, I knew you wanted me
to come here tonight. I just want to talk. To hold your hand. No seas
malita, dame un besito.* Her eyes dart, doorknob, three steps. He
snaps the light. *Shhh. Relax. I won't hurt you. Relax.*

Clouded dim moonlight
Eucalyptus tree branches
Tap against window

Urban Parrots

Some say it was a pet shop fire
in West Los Angeles during the great
mid-century Tiki craze.
Shopkeeper frantically opened cages.
Others say a truck filled with exotic birds
captured in Mayan jungles
took a curve on the 110 to Pasadena too fast.

I imagine planned escapes.
They watch for the precise moment
when doors and windows all open,
delicious first stretch of green wingspan
since capture in jungle canopy,
feathers tipped in dark blue like a pen nib,
calling out louder than a car horn
to other fugitives.

Unpacking boxes in a new apartment in Highland Park,
I hear them first, the sound of a tropical forest.
Parrots on the limbs of the backyard
mulberry tree, chatter to each other
in their green and red finery, practically camouflaged.
I stand transfixed at the window, heart full,
until in a burst, they fly. Daytime fireworks in a blue sky.

02: RELENTLESS LIFE

Elaine Mintzer

Botanic Garden Built Over a Landfill

Gluttonous bees stagger drunk on fragrance.
I drag my fingers along stem and leaf.

Mint and hyssop, sage and bergamot,
a riot of scent.

In a pond murky with algae
fish trouble the surface.

Saw-toothed succulents reach for sky.
Here and there a bike tire rises.

Tattered doll shoes poke like mushrooms
under notched palms.

Along my path, a few lifeless trees,
some spent flowers, a lost daughter.

How gaudy and enticing life is,
determined to be fruitful and multiply.

Buds, blooms, blossoms, bees surround me.
Beetles, snakes, spears and thorns.

Overhead, hawks circle.
At my feet, the shadows that precede them.

Amy Small-McKinney & Dick Westheimer

We Are What We Listen For

I sat with my anger long enough until she told me her real name was grief.

— C.S. Lewis

The air sings a murderous tune
heard only by cats and crows.

As the cat wanders away,
the air chants to a cunning of crows.

In the garden the corn sprouts,
is picked clean by a romance of crows.

What garden is this, filled
with withering roses and crows?

Fists and curses feed
those who misconstrue the crows.

The *Corvus* carries a note from the grave—
a message well known to crows.

There are three ways to avoid the cat's claws.
The first is to learn to love the call of crows.

Next, to listen to the air rain on the garden,
lifting the wings of crows.

Finally, the roses remind us of sorrow—
how Amy and Dick learn the language of crows.

Note: This poem, a ghazal, is a collaboration between two poets.

Hilda Weiss

Like the Parrots

It keeps showing up,
this glow inside me
somewhere.
It should be
religion, but
it's not. So
awkward . . .
to be glorified—
as it were,
as it seems,
as I am—
in this light.
Seeing it
open—
an aura,
aura-ing—
I disown it.
Still
it shows up
like these
squawky parrots
who come at night
to gather
in a chosen tree.

Aruni Wijesinghe

Disco Jesus

I find Christ
at the Purple Heart Thrift Store
at the hour of His arrival. When the girl
behind the counter lifts Him
from a box of donations, I know He
is mine. His shrink wrap is intact, His price
in Brazilian reales unsmudged on a blue sticker.
The chipped paint on His face and hands
gives Him a tortured saintliness,
but His stigmata are nail-polish bright.

What speaks to me most
is the mosaic of tiny mirrors
that adorn the drape of His robes.
Even through the dusty plastic shroud
He sparkles with diamond allure.
Tiffany splendor. Studio 54 fabulous.
I offer the princely sum of ten dollars,
carry him out the glass door with both hands,
admire him in the bright sun
of the strip mall parking lot.

At home I unwrap Him and place Him
in the center of the kitchen table.
After four years of marriage
my husband is used to my crow-like obsession
for anything shiny, shrugs at the treasures
I spirit home from second-hand store pilgrimages.
Jeff takes one glance at His glittering,
dubs Him Disco Jesus, then takes his mug of coffee
into another room. I sit on a chair, pew-hard,
rest my chin on double-stacked fists. I gaze
at hundreds of myselves reflected
in a nine-inch savior.

Disco Jesus finds His place
on the top shelf of our bar, outstretched arms
welcoming friends from between half-drunk bottles
of Hennessy and Crown Royal. Sometimes
I take Him down from His perch, wipe the dust
from His glory. I turn Him in my hands,
wonder at my own flawed appeal.

Revive

We are halfway through CPR training,
feeling confident about our abilities
to massage a phantom heart to the beat of
the Bee Gees' *Staying Alive* and breathe life
into polythene lungs when the instructor
begins distributing

babies. He circles the room, tells us which page
to turn to as he places a polypropylene infant
in front of every student. Each doll generates
an oddly satisfying thud as it lands. He begins
to review compressions per minute
but I am distracted by

a pink onesie embroidered with flowers.
My manikin looks cold. I swaddle her
in my sweatshirt, tuck the sleeves
around her small body and shrug the hood
over her tiny head. One day I will crochet her
a blanket in soft colors and a scalloped border.

I practice the breath of life. Watch for the rise
and fall of a doll chest, chafe hands and feet
for some sign of revival. While the others practice
anti-choking maneuvers, I cradle this inert body
assigned to me to save. I heft her weight
onto my shoulder, pat her back and coo,

try to comfort
myself.

03: DYING ALIVE

Nancy Beagle

Eyes on Music

Reinvention

Nathaniel Dolton-Thornton

aether/oar

There is a Great Year, whose winter is a great flood and whose summer is a world conflagration. In these alternating periods the world is now going up in flames, now turning to water.

— *Heraclitus, On Nature*

winter: XLVI

the restaurant parking lot is a marina
headlights drift, harbor buoys

gulls thread tendons in the sky's arm
shrieking when it tenses

I beat pots and pans
so I can't hear myself think

for other reasons than the storm
when I squint, stillness shivers

winter: LXXI

the boat drags, a sea slug
over sea slugs through water

island houses all look the same
in their variety: patterned tiles, vibrant colors

clam diggers used to sell clams
now they sell photos of clam diggers

every muscle feels
the tense we live in

winter: LXXII

the gull must've died yesterday
or the day before

I sit out of sight
and upwind from it

its wings clutch kelp like
kelp clutches its wings like

a fetid Celtic knot
the beer bottle lies most naturally

should we mourn the loss
of weeds we've pulled?

winter: LXXIII

I liked the irises so much
better after frostbite

some mornings it's painful
to see anything grow

crowds in empty bleachers
have a good cry without me

the one-eyed squirrel doesn't
need the peanut man's call to answer

winter: LXXIV

in this tumbledown coastal town
every house names itself

after somewhere else—
Cornwall, Tuscany, Greece—

even the paint's glazed over
under scolding, watching gulls

rest, and flare, and rest
imitating midlife crises

I feel almost
but not quite at home here, like most residents

Lesley Rogers Hobbs

~~House For Sale:~~ SOLD

Snow falls; large flakes and whirling flurries,
full of delight until they disappear

into the wet earth. The dog barks
in frustration, cheated of the chase,

a scraggly brown lawn sprinkled liberally
with deer shit and mole hills—perhaps

spring will be verdant; should I plant
in hopeful abandon or proceed cautiously

uncertain what this new place holds?
Yet another beginning; I'm tired of forced

enthusiasm, tired of starting over with
4-inch pots, bare-root promises and paint samples

that are never quite what I want.

Rachel Neve Midbar

The Demon You Read

You read your mother on notices nailed to random trees or on sheets
billowing in the breeze, pinned to lines outside and meant to dry.
You read her in the poems written by Tibetin monks, their saffron
robes spicing the stanzas, their red sashes, the silences between. You
read your mother in the mirror, on the crosshatched skin of your
neck, Once, but only once, you pushed your head out from between
her thighs as she lay sleeping, just as she is sleeping now, in the
twilight of her life, her soft snores cowering under the slump of her
breasts. You are sliced when they bring their shame to slit you, the
roundness that claims you like an unwashed cup. You read yourself
there too, turned upside down, a dybbuk aswim in your grounds. She
lies there, unshattered, her hair split under her crown, her seaweed
feet, her mermaid body, eyes round around and empty as a cup,
empty as her arms that she has wrapped tight under her nipples. Is
she your mother? The one who has come undone? Or isn't that just
you?

Chanel Brenner

Let's Keep the Cat

Because he wandered into our dark
hearts and backyard,

the day Jupiter aligned with the sun,
radiating his luck upon us.

Because his moonstone eyes
promise new beginnings,

and his fur coat is a melange
of banana bread and Neapolitan ice cream
that satiates our sweet tooth.

Let's keep the cat,
because of mountain peaks,

expansive green fields,
and footballs soaring through air,

because he roams our yard like a lion,
and makes us want to dance
on our tails like dolphins in ocean spray.

Let's keep the cat,
because of gravel that spits
a pebble into a shoe to bother a foot,

because of pools bereft of water,
but filled with sand, and broken shells
that jab like judgment.

Let's rainbow him with love,
shower him with wisteria
and seabream!

Let's wave a hundred flags for him,
hire a pilot to skywrite his name,
tell the world he is ours!

But first let's name her.

Exit Way

When I'm not writing,
I watch the ant crawl
up the wall.

When the gardener trims
our ficus to its bones
I wonder how it feels
to be that exposed.

When I walk,
I talk to the dead,
and tree-cloaked branches
shadow me.

When I check the crack
in our pitched wood ceiling
and it weeps, I wipe the sap
like a child's nose.

When I stare at the rust stain
in our driveway, an imprint
from a piece of wood,
left behind in the rain,

I wonder, what else remains.

The crushed dent in the tile
from an accident
I don't remember happening—
or something more unknowable.

When I see the bull's eye gong
in the doorway, I wonder
if it's an entryway or an exit way,
as its echo bells my bones,

with a ringing too hollow
to ever fill.

Rachel Walker

Half-Ghost

My dreams are full of arguments with you:
we stand on tables and chairs and look down
at the splintering floorboard, the long cracks
in the ceiling. A mouse shakes the table
at the corner of my dream, rattling
porcelain teacups and throwing the smell
of rosehips across the room. We close our eyes
and count to three. A teacup shatters. When
you leave, the walls are covered in notes
on bright paper. They droop like daffodils.
Your handwriting is my own. *Like a mouse,*
you wrote, *I am crawling towards nowhere*
in particular. I wake with a mouth stained
green, memory of earth against my teeth.

Aleksandra Scepanovic

Lost

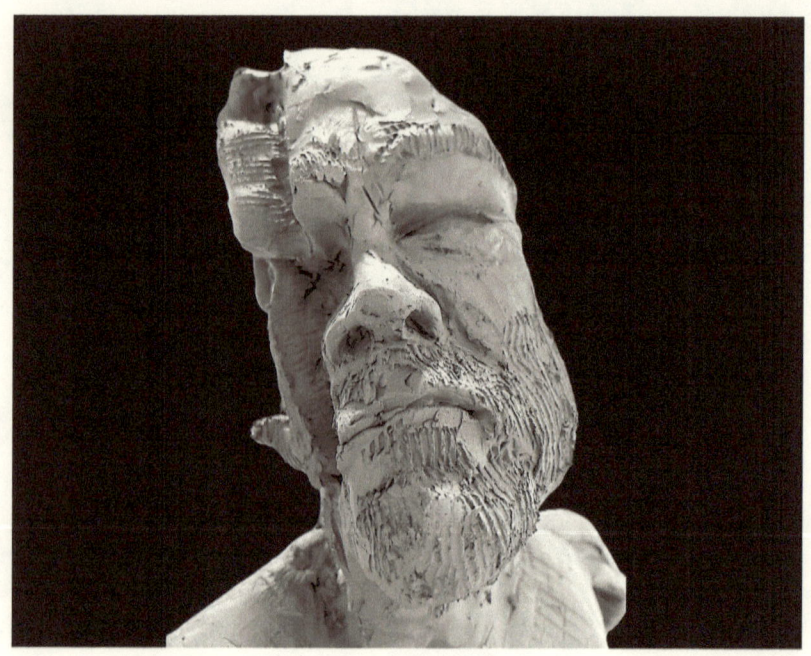

The Vanishing

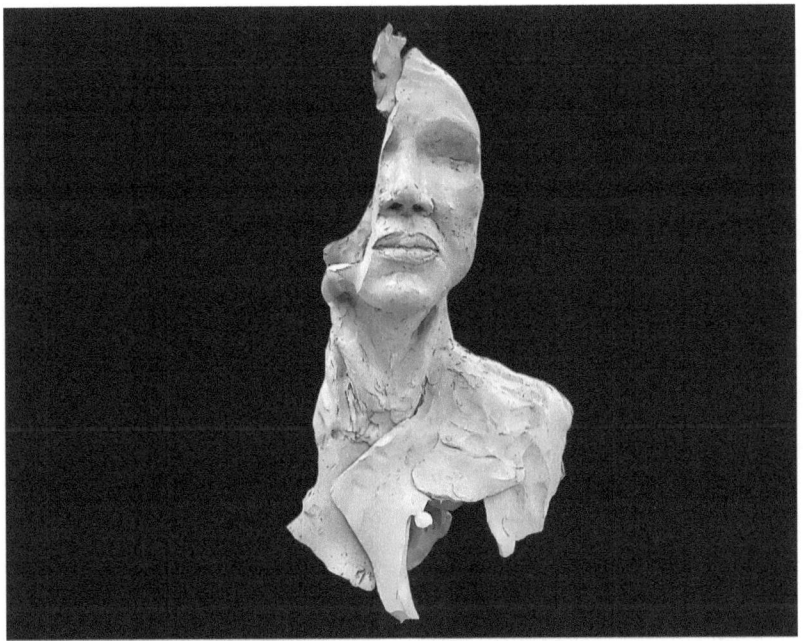

Michael J. Galko

A week in Japan as a smoker

I knew my marriage would die.
We were here in March, watching it fade.
I had to stop drinking first.
But I knew it would still die, once I stopped.

I was back in Tokyo in October, alone.
I found a pack of cigarettes
in the back seat of the cab from Narita.
It was full. I put it in my jacket.

I was the only flyperson at the meeting.
So I was a curiosity, even more
than your average westerner in Japan.
During the breaks, I taught myself

to smoke. I can see now
why cigarettes are a staple
of AA meetings. They reduce
the inevitable cravings.

In the evening, I would jog
in slow sorrow around the Imperial
Palace, as the dusk brightened
the traffic lights on the roads.

I have never been able
to pick up a woman, apropos
solely of desire. This held true
for my Japanese smoking phase.

There was a young woman there I liked.
She wore smart skirts and blouses.
I went to her poster. Her accent
was Australian. She was flirty.

I certainly desired her. She'd watch me,
as I lit up after my evening jog,
she heading to dinner with colleagues.
I thought I saw her nod,

as if to say, come along with us.
I was faithful, all through my marriage,
for reasons that still perplex me.
I quit drinking, an ember at my fingertips.

Gahl Liberzon

Post-Mortum

On the plane back to Chicago
from my now dead vacation, a trip
inherited from my dead grandmother, I read

a book of poems by the favorite dead author
of my dead best friend. What is it like?
The surviving? The going-on?

I smell the recycled air. It goes on.
I look out the window
at the wing, the clouds. They go on.

Up ahead, my grandfather sits
in first class, eating cashews and almonds,
thinking inscrutable grandfatherly thoughts

and napping when the spirit moves him.
He goes on famously. He has
since the first of his wars, back

when he was seventeen. None of us
are quite sure if it makes us
brothers or witnesses, so

we do not speak of it. Dead is dead.
I don't know what I would say.
The greatest respect I know

is not to salt the wound
or rock the boat. Once, after
a nearly fatal traffic accident,

after I'd gotten out of the car
that crumpled like an accordion,
I did a little jig. Once,

after I got the folks to call
the ambulance, I looked at
my hands. It's like that too. *Still*

Here you think, just as the clouds think
the same thing, curling in on themselves.
Then they turn to look at you

as you turn to look up at them. *Still There.*
And then, what else can you do?
One foot in front of the next.

Todd Robinson

I See Her from the Spare Bedroom

Green eyes bright with medicine, baking bison at 3 AM again, gabapentin high, pale feet bare on gritty kitchen tile, tardy snow weighing the chokecherry tree's branches, her clatter and fester. Six years sick since the lumbar puncture, the PICC line, insane ingenuities to keep her throat catching with hope. I am a minotaur huffing on a greasy pillow, so selfish I could swallow oceans to get a single scallop, eat the nacre from her gnarled heart, my favorite habit. *An agoraphobe loves the house they'll die in, destroy-before-abandon,* Carson Young writes, a diagnosis for two strangers in stasis. Is this self-supervised home hospice, or just two more ringside seats to eternity? No answer from tinnitus and HVAC wheeze. Only the drip of a soggy joist at 4 AM. I vow to call another roofer, another plumber, fix the rot. Vampire in a spare casket, undead poet tonguing a fang. 5 AM, under the burned out kitchen track lights, she says there is a pain so great you feel the universe's malice. *Please Van Gogh my ear, dear.* I eye the knife rack, weigh our ache, the moon through skylight glass pummeled to silica, a silence so total it disproves gods. I am afraid of love's half-life, perfect blue icebergs calving in my skull. I love you, top-knot. I love you, silk pajamas. In laying these words at her flower feet the seconds become sunlight—warm the empty air between us, the ruined hours of our braided life.

04: INOPERABLE

Ron Koertge

ICU

I rush my snowman
to the hospital.
Broken nose
replaced by a carrot.
Corneal surgery with
Hershey's kisses.
But nothing can be
done
about spring.

The Prophet Isaiah

urged warriors to beat their swords into ploughshares. Everybody
liked Isaiah and he had a hotline to God. So they - the warriors -
went to work at the forge. That was fun all sweaty with their mates
again, home in time for dinner, play with the kids. But it turned out
that what Isaiah and Yahweh had in mind wasn't just turning swords
into ploughshares but then plowing with them and getting oxen
shit on those cool sandals that lace up tanned-and-powerful calves.
The warriors didn't want to be farmers and they told Isaiah so.
Isaiah said. "Look. Swords are tools of destruction and ploughshares
are tools that benefit mankind." The warriors said, "We liked our
swords." And what did Isaiah do all day but sit around stroking his
beard and prophesying while the farmers came and complained
that all the warriors wanted to do was take off their clothes and
wrestle then polish their armor. Things were getting heated when
a messenger arrived with news that the enemy - the hot-blooded,
rapacious enemy - was headed their way. While the farmers hid
behind haystacks or disguised themselves as scarecrows and Isaiah
prayed at the top of his lungs, the warriors found that the sun off
the new ploughshares blinded the enemy and made them easy to
slaughter using the razor-sharp edges that reminded them of their
beloved swords.

Therese Gleason

In the Negative

It was my brother, not me
who saw my father die—
but I couldn't stop picturing him

in the driveway, eyes open,
unseeing gaze cast to the sky.
Three months later, in the black

and white photos from my wedding,
I smiled beside my groom
as if talking in my sleep,

my eyes shut in every shot.
I must have sensed the flash
as it happened, migraineur that I am,

hypersensitive to light.
Or did I clamp
my lids closed against

my father's absence,
willing him to emerge
blinding white, in the negative

behind my eyes?
It was a morning wedding
and a mourning wedding;

a magical day of magical thinking:
if my father's spirit
could leave his body

in the time it takes to blink,
who's to say I couldn't
conjure him back

the same way?

Nancy Beagle

Let the Fish Go?
after Elizabeth Bishop

In me she has drowned a young girl, and in me an old woman
Rises toward her day after day, like a terrible fish.

— *Sylvia Plath*

I try shoving that fish into the placid lake
No gentle letting go. I don't want it with its
brown skin, creased and wrinkled like ancient
wallpaper. Its gills breathing in and out,
its popping eyes, bloodshot, irises yellowed.
My sullen face meets me, unacceptable
sheen of night sweat, lower lip dotted
with drool, hanging like an old piece
of fishing-line. All the trophies of aging--
medals with their ribbons tattered--
the protruding veins, the discolored
flesh, the warts, skin tabs--all testament
to years of treading water, fighting currents,
swimming upstream.

Was the getting here victory? Does it
fill up this rented boat, as Bishop claims?
Is there any gold pot at the end of the rainbow?
That terrible fish, tremendous fish, rising day
by day, its mouth grim, wet, sucking what pap
is still to be found. I have no beard of wisdom,
only a mustache that sprouts wayward hairs,
resistant to the blade. I see no victory
crowding this boat. It is going down. Down.
This old woman greets me, this terrible fish

pulling at breath strings, pulling me toward
inevitable end. Take the hook from my mouth,
stack the medals by the door, stare and stare
as the fish rises, rises.

Patricia Davis-Muffett

What It's Like to Be Human

You will walk barefoot around your dry winter house
all day. Over time, your feet will callous and crack.
You will go to the nail salon at the strip mall
and just when you close your eyes and exhale,
the little girl in the chair beside you will glimpse
the cheese grater grinding your feet and gasp.
You will live in half a room. Or you will live
in five rooms, when two would be enough.
Your cat and beloved dog will die. You will walk
down a street you have walked a thousand times
and a dog you've never met will lick your face.
A cat with a limp will follow you home and claim you.
You will mean to make that phone call, return
that email. More often than not, you will fail.
Some days, you will hold a clipboard in hand,
tuck a pencil behind your ear, and take on the world.
Some days, you will lay on the floor face down
and wonder how you'll ever get up. Some days,
if you're lucky, someone will sit down on that
hard floor, stroke your hair as your mother did,
maybe even rub your calloused feet and say,
It's ok. Let's just stay here. I will bring you
a cup of tea. I'll add a few grains of salt
to make it taste less bitter.

Patricia L. Scruggs

Bones, Them Cracked Bones

We are all held together
by Scotch Tape, my friend says.
And sometimes, Super Glue.

My fibula. Cracked.
Spent two and a half weeks
in a temporary splint—

felt like I was in old Western
where they used
long pieces of kindling

and a strip torn from
the hem of my petticoat
to hold the bone in place.

Now at last, I have
a walking boot
that releases me

from the crutches,
while reminding me
I am not invulnerable.

Best to move this pen
across the page
while the mind holds

and the body
remains upright.
My scaffolding

is wearing down.
I need
a bigger roll

of Scotch Tape
to hold it together.

Car Sick

6,000 miles in the back of a woody station wagon.
The heat of summer in every direction. The back
end swerved like my stepfather through
our lives. A vertiginous wisdom
and parallel imprisonment.
Seldom up close but with force.
Always according to his temper
and timeline Always an appointment
to keep, blood to draw, boil to lance. Another file
to write, gotta keep up daily, get up nightly,
another baby to birth, another spine to tap,
an argument to win. Boy, the classics love a good
argument. Can make you believe black is the new blue,
and brown is the best barn red. This is Plato, Balzac
or Rabelais, instead of a book club romance,
or a meat plate special A child
born from his mother's left ear. Trace
that birth canal through eternity's assumptions.
I'm no scientist or mathematician. A Buddhist by
nature. Catholic by association. Jewish by
heritage. Call me dervishly inclined. Religi-
ossically curious—to the far clean bones of
all one hundred twenty-six *Samdhi* rules,
a devotee of Saraswati, a juggler of
Devanagari, a student of *Asteya* and
Vinyasa Krama, cognizant of all four *Padas,*
a practitioner of wind and motion.
I am a future absence, this present tense,
Here. While the world hangs on a storm.

Amanda Le

That Which Was Forgotten

Postmortem

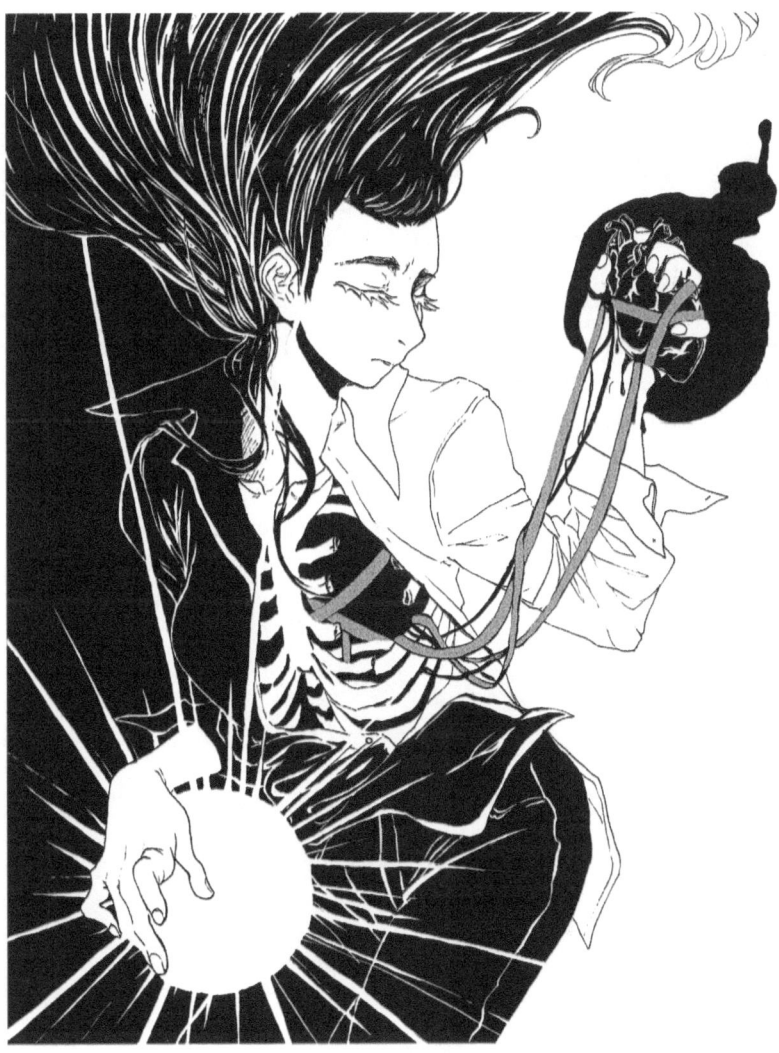

Alexis Rhone Fancher

The God for Broken People

There is a god for broken people

— *Roxane Gay*

This is the god for the second rate, the one who waylays you at the
party, plies you with bourbon, fucks you in the kitchen, makes
you walk home in the rain. This god shines in the run off. This
god hustles the night. This god mines the maimed, culls emotional
cripples off the top like cream. This god is a shape-shifter, a dumpster
diver, the god who loiters at the corner of Dolorosa & Despair.
This god drinks alone. The god for broken people trolls the city for
discards, marries the exploited with the lost. This god sweeps up
the miscreants, gusts their darkness into night. This is the god of
no hope. No money. This god has your back when you backslide.
This god bets on you to fail, hides in your broken places. This god is
willing to wait. When you're ready to surrender, remember: this is
your last, best chance. This god will not stick by you, won't give you
false hope. This god will kill you. Or save you. Choose.

05: BLIND AWAKENING

Yvette R. Murray

After Hearing the Truth, Woman Walks Alone in the Fog

Fog sits on a city   like a hand over an open mouth
desperate for silence   screaming from the eyes
It finds no peace   I find no peace
wrapping around streetlights   after the runaway
runs away into itself   starts to break apart
and finds another space   to begin anew
again begins to crawl   all through a city
dances with smoke   like the forgotten note
mesmerizing silent ode   to nothingness
all alone with itself   roams a tangled bramble
drowns again in the air   cuts within
the reign of grey ends   heals with prayer
vanishes each to each   into inner space
yields to the sun   blooms an orange grace.

Legacy

I was born with ears that stand out from my head,
twin satellite dishes, ready to snatch signals from the air.
They were a sign I would inherit the family deafness.
And I did, though it took time. The ears themselves
look fine, spiraling like galaxies. But not hearing
makes most conversation awkward. I must fill in blanks
as best I can; connection wanes. As the world outside
grows still, the one within gets louder, until my dreams
begin to swell into a symphony. Drifting off to sleep,
my sound-starved brain composes melodies.
I'm marooned within a muffled world I don't know how
to navigate. Perhaps, like my grandmother, I'll turn
everyone into interpreters, one day myself become
a guide, mapping the route for others trapped in newly
silent worlds. rather than sliding, as my mother did,
into rivers of music only she could hear, losing sight
of land, drifting entirely away.

Golden Shovel, from a line by Emily Dickinson

I won't keep secrets, try always to tell
hard truths before they weigh me down. All
the scandals others stash or burn or bury in the
attic, lock in a trunk and throw away the key. Truth
can disinfect. It may disappoint or shock, but
the buried secret will surface anyway, will tell
itself like an unmarked grave. I know it
from experience, how secrets set a life a-slant.

Brian Sonia-Wallace

Grace

You are at work & I am sleeping with my neighbor:
half boredom, half revenge. A habit, really.
The universe is exploding outward,
the edges dark because, there, back in time
(we're always looking back in time, in space) gravity
is so dense even the light from the Big Bang
can't escape. We adjust our definitions,
glasses, expectations, barbell weights,
meeting times, how we sleep on each others '
numb arms. We — that's something
we still believe in, right? A forgiveness
that started years ago, still expanding.

Instructions for Living

In tarot, the death card means new
beginnings, rebirth. Chromosomes
come paired, too, father-mother split,
each of us a profane hybridity —
look, this sinew is what's left
of your forefathers,
go
gently.
Let the flesh be young & then
eat salt until it becomes salt.
Start something. Bread. A cult. A novel.
A way of seeing. Keep
starting, jagged, limping. Death
is the lame uncle who always comes
too early. You are still getting
ready. Make smalltalk. Buy time.

Terri Niccum

Relinquished

I've given up reading palms,
shilling those with open faces,
their hands stretched toward me
splayed like fish,
fingers grasping for a somewhere
to point to.

I've given up claiming
a knowledge of lifelines
and nurturing clients' belief
in my deeper sight,
in my ability to dowse
water and fortunes.

I've given up the slick
feel of cards sliding below
my fingers,
the sense that my fingers
could beckon any card.

I've stopped stoking
false hope – even though
they beg me, tell me any hope
is better than none.

I've given up
practicing tricks and replacing –
with forced adeptness –
honest despair with any
coin that glitters.

I've given up pretense
to earn dark meaning,
to mouth it like
an abscessed tooth.
To hold emptiness in my being
like a vacant building
houses shadow.

I've stopped saying the right thing
and now clamp my lips
and listen for truth
in the earth's quaking.
Find balance in the rephrasing
of an old quarrel.
Bracing, righting myself.

Inferno

I burn the way money burns

— Anne Sexton

Like a poor man's dreams, or a rich man's idle hands.
I am at times desperation, at other times boredom.
In the dark I tear the world down
that the fools among you should feel my contempt.
In the light I am revolution.
I build so that what should be
becomes what is.

Jane Zich

Spirit of Renewal

Revision

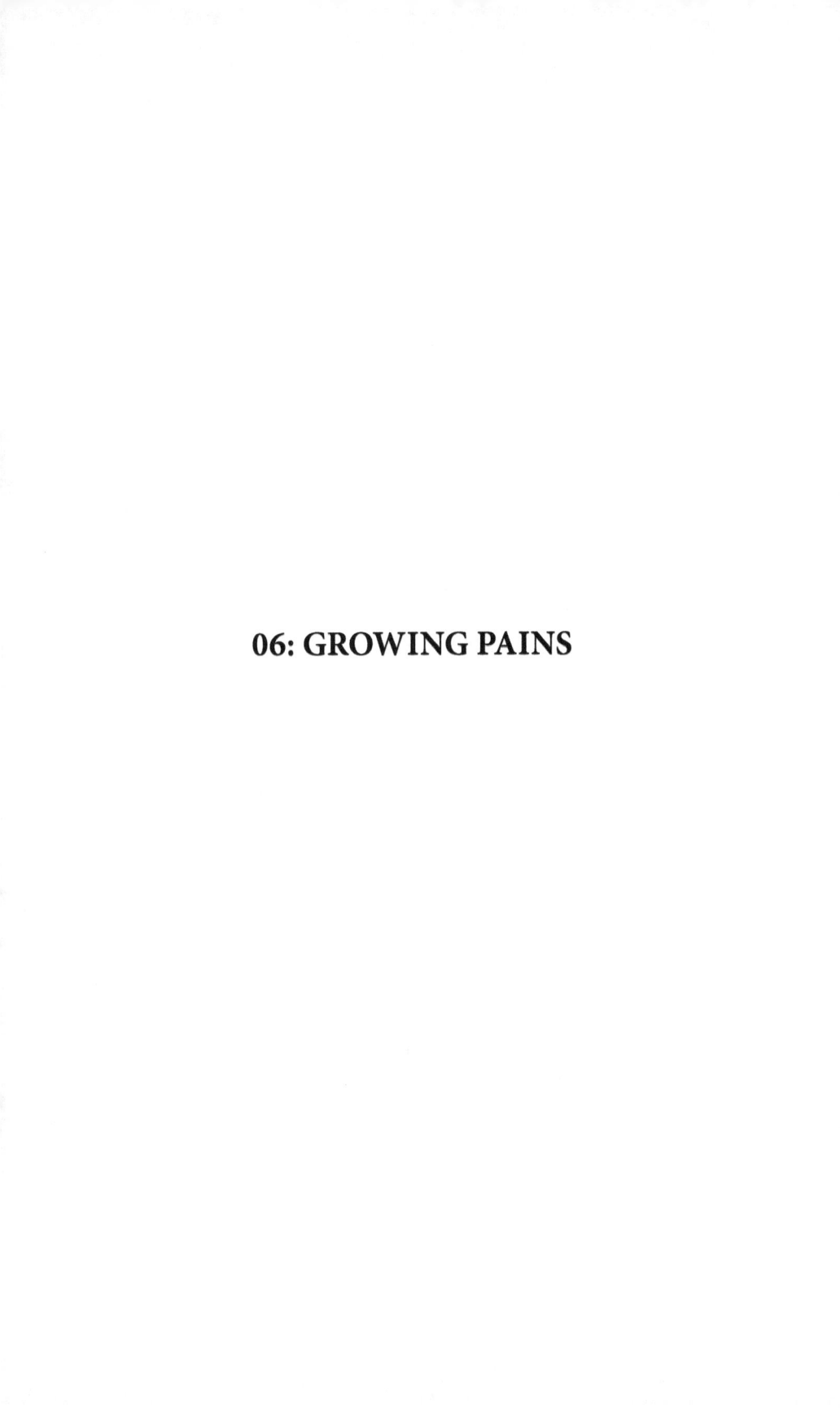

06: GROWING PAINS

Charles Harper Webb

Dissection Day

A cow's eyeball is big enough for two
students to share. When Mrs. Park says,

"Decide among you who'll do what,"
Al, who plans to be a doctor, grabs

a knife, and hands a bib to glowering
metal-head Brad. "You can take notes."

Brad glares. "*You* take the notes."
Al says, "No way." Brad—a foot taller—

leans into him. His stubbled chin sand-
papers Al's beardless face, which refuses

to retreat as classmates surge to see.
"Gimme the blade," Brad snarls. "Pussy."

Gnats of spit smack into Al, who pipes,
"Why come so close? You want to kiss me?"

Classmates' eyes go dodgeball-huge.
Blasts of laughter napalm Brad.

As Mrs. Park runs up in slow, slow motion,
Brad gives Al a shove worth three days'

suspension. Al rebounds off the wall
with, "Dude, that's some harsh b.o."

For the first time at school, Al is a hero.
No one thinks, next day, of Brad, his dad's

Glock stuffed in his backpack, bullets
stacked in the clip, glinting like rat-eyes.

Alexis Rhone Fancher

Walking on Water

I'm Not Poisonous, I'm Just Drawn that Way

Michael Juliani

Amazing Grace, Imagine, Hallelujah

One year, when the Olympics flashed on TV,
        you slipped on the living room's
oily Persian rug. A dozen family members watched the end
        of the race while you bled. Your mother brought you
ice water to keep you awake, tucking your toy
        rifle into bed next to you, the sags
of her body and your father's widening the aperture
        of the shock. Fifteen years later, you find yourself pinned down
in a wilderness camp somewhere outside Provo. You have a broken
camera,
        a CD player, and a bag of dirty loose change
to your name. You feed the horses apples, you pet the dogs,
        you paint whales on tiny canvas. Your father visits
wearing black. Your mother chokes words out
        like she's under arrest. It's cold all five months.
Your promises and diaries are jokes: you describe a girl
        combing her hair topless in a rainforest, eighty thousand
screaming girls with their dresses flung
        over their heads. You swallow three cups of red punch
and sneak twelve packets of sugar, and the staff
        puts a sticker beside your name
labeling what new problem you are. They make you
        feel like a pale little boy trying to learn
how to deny himself with words. The Utah stars are opened butterfly
        knives on sale in Chinatown, throbs of the old
bus routes you took. At your roommate's graduation,
        they hand out ukuleles and pocket Boggle,
everyone singing Amazing Grace, Imagine,
        Hallelujah. He's flying home to New Jersey by himself,
wearing a new pair of Vans, no longer frilled
        with Sharpie-drawn pot leaves and swastikas.

You know it doesn't mean he hates
        any less, but you promise to live together
when you turn eighteen, without cell phones
        for your parents to track. Then you see your AA sponsor,
a man a little younger than your father
        who smiles at everything that comes out
of your mouth—how you love watching TV
        at your girlfriend's house while she and her parents
are at work, how leisure is the top principle
        of your life, how the freshly washed bed sheets
smell like turpentine.

Saul Bernstein

The ultimate arrogance: to rename yourself.
Your father said he did it for you,
for your future: traded Bernstein for Behrens.

You were 15, already bar mitzvahed,
instructed in religious law, when he stripped
you of your birth name. Who had you lost?

Your mother lost two names when he took
away the one he'd given her in marriage.
For your father it was not enough to stress

the "i," to be a Bern *stine* like Lenny. No,
your father took the big step, like the leap
Jerome Rabinowitz took to Jerry Robbins.

And you, who'd been left out of the decision,
you later claimed it, put your name into type
in newspapers, in theater programs, moved it

from the back pages of the paper to front page
by-lines, to magazines—made yourself a name
in a way your father never had as Bernstein.

And the change from Saul? That was all you.
Later, you thought all of it was your idea:
turning from Judaism, dating Christian girls.

You thought your parents didn't approve.
But really, all those years ago, wasn't it
your father, pushing you toward me?

Susan Hayden

I Didn't Know How to Twist

or shout. But in 1984 on a Tuesday night at The Boss Club at Imperial Gardens on Sunset Boulevard, I tried to do both.

I'd tricked this guy from my acting class, Bobby Sugarman, into asking me out. He had dark tousled curls, hypnotist's eyes and wore a jean vest, checked flannel shirt with cut-off sleeves and bandana as headband. He could have been Springsteen's baby brother.

So why did "Twist and Shout" have to be playing instead of "Back In Your Arms Again"? I wanted to slow dance with Bobby Sugarman but Bruce's cover had turned The Boss Club into American Bandstand and everyone was grinding, thrusting, swaying.

"Rotate your hips, your torso. Bend your elbows. Go low," Bobby instructed, his hands finally on me, even though you weren't supposed to touch the other person in this dance. "Everything moves but stay put."

"I'm trying," I told him.

"It's like playing Twister without your feet," he said, encircling me with his moves while I stood there, flailing.

I was from Encino not New Jersey. I'd graduated from the mellow sound to loving punk. The only dancing I'd ever done was slow and at bar mitzvahs or jumping wildly in a mosh-pit.

I'd been studying Bobby Sugarman for months, every Monday night in Matt Chait's acting workshop in a black box on Santa Monica Boulevard and Vine at the Richmond Shepard Theatre. He was a born actor, had technique *and* charisma, was teacher's pet.

Across the hallway, at the same time, Exene happened to be taking voice lessons with Gloria Bennett. I'd hold my ear up to the door and listen to her warm-up exercises. She was my mascot in those days. She stood for all I had never known.

And in class, I'd attempt to present another excerpt from Studs Terkel's collection, "Working." Every young actor I'd ever met performed from that book. There was the waitress, the auditor, the steelworker, the gravedigger, the bookbinder.

I chose the "New York hooker." The opening line of my monologue was: "A hustler is any woman in American society." I was 21 and picked the piece for shock value. I knew nothing about being a woman or the working life in its many forms.

Matt Chait told me to relax. "Take off your shoes, rub your feet. Find the original wound and speak from it," he said.

Bobby Sugarman used my time on stage to go outside and smoke. His original wound had colored lights and a megaphone. He only stayed in class when he was onstage or when one of his friends was doing a scene.

Why was I in this workshop, anyway? I blamed it on a celebrity psychic I met when I was nine, who'd told me I was going to grow up to be a famous actress. This was the same psychic who predicted Sharon Tate's killer was "a man with a beard named Charlie."

So I spent my days reading plays by Tennessee Williams, James Kirkwood Jr. and Beth Henley. At night I'd go to punk clubs to hear X, The Weirdos and The Germs, where you didn't need to know how to twist, only meld.

Springsteen belonged to high school, to stadium days, the phase where we slept in front of Ticketron at Topanga Plaza to get floor seats to The River tour. It was behind me now. But a night with Bobby Sugarman had been more my goal in acting class than learning an actual craft. And if he loved Springsteen, I was willing to look back.

How did I get so lucky as to finally make it happen? By telling him, after he'd finished a masterful scene from "Death of a Salesman," that I knew someone in the business who could help him.

"Oh, really? Why don't you come with me to The Boss Club next week and we can discuss?" Bobby suggested.

He had never talked to me in class before I'd approached him. And it was true, I answered phones in my father's office where a personal manager of actors rented space in the same suite. We were friends and he sometimes listened to my suggestions.

I had eight days notice to starve myself on grapefruit and hard boiled eggs, lose eight pounds, buy red stilettos at Leeds in Fashion Square, get a perm to make my curls more defined, and squeeze into Big Joe jeans by laying on the floor and holding my breath.

This was the 80s and I didn't believe in myself yet. At The Boss Club, I used my body as a 3-speed oscillating fan, trying to twist, like the biggest geek in a John Hughes movie waiting to be written.

Bobby Sugarman was twisted in front me. He knew all the moves, the words to every Springsteen song, And just like in acting class, he emanated ease and sparkle, he glowed center stage. It would be the closest I ever came to dancing with Springsteen.

"So you don't know how to act *or* dance?" he blurted out on the ride home.

But that didn't stop him from wanting to make out with me, even as he said, "I feel weird doing this because I have a sister named Susan." He called me the next day, not to say what a good time he'd had but to ask when he could connect with my manager friend. I set it up and they met for coffee *that week*. The manager later remarked, "Sweet kid but he's just another Springsteen wannabe."

On Monday night, I drove to the acting studio on Santa Monica and Vine but decided when I got there to skip class. I thought, maybe I'll even quit studying here. No one in the room sees my potential.

I did climb the stairs to Gloria Bennett's voice studio and held my ear to the door. I could hear Exene's growls turning smooth and almost smoky. I wanted her to stop. I loved her original singing, raw and untrained. Yet she was committed to growing. To being more. I was too but you'd never have known it.

I didn't know how to twist or shout, act or dance. But I knew that soon I would find my own natural voice. And I would do it without taking lessons.

J.D. Isip

Homing

Give a thing a story and it is no longer a thing.
Pigeons, a friend tells me, once carried messages
from castles and their lovelorn inhabitants. Mail
by way of their once-lovely wings, the abalone
shimmer a meaning before the words. Eager
hands reached out for them, welcomed them.

What became of these flying Grizabellas? A story
she heard that winged its way along the internet
is one we all know too well: what was named
and loved lost its use and, thus, its purpose, was
cast aside to scurry and scrounge to survive. Yet,
they multiply, tar and feather every city surface.

Fate cannot conquer what takes her condemnation,
her crusts and sludge, and shit it back on creation.

The Myth of the Magikarp
or, When I Was a Straight Woman

When someone tells you who they are, so it goes,
you should believe them, and so I did. I believed
the fish-like monsters, their round mouths pulling
in air, pulling in someone like me with their spell
that makes one believe they will get bigger

someday, they say, they will get bigger, the catch
was, of course, I would have to accept them now,
small and flaccid and unfulfilling, and not alone,
but with more of their kind, dozens, maybe more,
but, they would say, it will be worth it—

so I believed their stories about what they could be,
a sleek, serpentine, powerful beast, one I could ride
for the rest of our lives, their muscles contracting
between these thighs, the thighs where they'd sleep
in their unchanged form, deathlike and cold—

by the time I was on Magikarp number 200 or so,
there she was singing along with her Jigglypuff,
and she looked at me with the fish, got quiet, sad,
and asked me how many I had, and when I told her,
she said you'll need two times more, and trust me

she said, what you get is not what you've heard,
not what they promised you, the power, the waves
they say you'll glide across, the rush of the ocean,
and she took my hand, pushing the fish away, here,
wiggling her fingers in mine, I'll teach you to sing.

Edward Garza

Andre in the Cave

07: UTTERANCE

Mariano Zaro

The Mercy of Memory

Cúbrete la cicatriz. Le dicen.
There is a scar.

> Her right elbow shattered in a car accident,
> a ski accident, perhaps the non-accident of war.

There is also a platinum plate,
and two screws.

> She wears long sleeves,
> even in the summer months.
> *Pero no te quejes.* Le dicen.

Don't say "screws," say "pins." It's softer.
Somebody recommends.

> She doesn't go to the pool,
> to the beach. Doesn't go out much.

The first known use of the word "scar"
was in the 14th century.

> *¿Sabes que "cicatrix" es también*
> *una palabra en inglés?* Le dicen.

As if a scar could have a nationality.

> One night,
> she wears a sleeveless dress.

What happened to you? she is asked.
It's nothing, she says.
I'm not good with etymologies.

And she covers the scar
with her constant embroidery of silk
and small daily consolations.

Lao Rubert

Words Are Not

Words are not a vaccine,
not a roof or a repair to the wiring,
not a jump to the electrical system.
Words are not a tree,
not a marathon, or a physical therapist,
not a dinner with risotto
or a summer melon.
They are not a ladybug, a firefly or cardinal,
not headphone or translation.
Words don't feed an aging parent,
don't help her dress,
don't cool a summer day,
but words can be a lotion, a hot drink
that picks the body up,
prepares it to live again—
the reason to risk the trek,
the song to sing while walking.

Shirley J. Brewer

Poem Beginning with a Line from Richard Hugo

*You might come here Sunday on a whim,
after a whiskey sour brunch in Hampden
where everyone calls you *Hon.*
Witness the bold explosion. Isn't it rich
the way a woman revives her life?
Feast on feathery red lamps, a flamingo-
pink coffee table, lime pillows.
Light splashes in through tall windows.
Lavender high heels sequin the mantel.
Listen to the vibrant sounds
of sirens and the city.
You might wonder how someone
could move forward and away
from all the canyons of the past,
without a map, without a plan.

* "Degrees of Gray in Philipsburg"

Joanne Clarkson

Daring the Re-Discovered Life

My friend, the newly minted hypnotist,
offers to give me a day of my life
over. To charm my mind into memory
and re-awaken a younger self. I can choose
any day. At first this sounds
wonderful – to re-capture a tango
of joy, the exaltation of achievement,
conversations or the tremor of reciprocal
touch. Then, as if pricked by a thorn,
I recall the disbelief within all
happiness. The unworthiness shadowing
honors. And how could I risk caress
when I know it will be taken away?
He is surprised when I tell him
No thank you. A little hurt, so proud
is he of his mastery of timelessness.
Over the next few days, my memory
does seem ignited. At unlikely times
I get a flash of Paris or a crimson sky.
I taste the shiver of an unripe seaside
berry. Feel the seductive fingers
offering it. Open my mouth this time.

Trish Holden

On the Way

Brian Duran-Fuentes

The Returned

At sundown my children return on horseback,
sleep bites their faces riding up the prairie,
paper knights with margins crimson and faded.
Their hands are empty.

I boil water for soup and sharpen pencils,
the congealed ink spirals down the tip of the pen.
The world is hard to conquer, but that is ok.
my poems are safe.

Laocoon, cancer-ridden, three headed bastard,
Hellborn penguin sporting a top hat and cane,
sleep deprived Persephone on her lunch break;
the three of them stare.

They lay down their headers on throw pillows,
their artifices hang by the windowsill,
I brush their syntax and put cream on their feet.
they rinse with mezcal.

Morning comes like the new draft for an email.
My poems set out on their conquest again.
May at least one of them bloom victorious,
as pollen adrift.

LeAnne Hunt

Idaho

The cows are lowing.
My husband said it is weaning time,
the calves taken from their mothers.
Next morning, Jen remarks that it sounded
like older cows calling
and the younger calling back.

Over and over, I wake to cows lowing.
I sent my daughter away
to help her.
She wanted to go, but not to this place—
the desert, the heat, the dust,
pit foot and bad food.

The cows are so loud
as if our tent were surrounded by grieving mothers
and their lost children.
My daughter is on a cot next to me,
so close I can hear her rustling through sleep.
On my other side, her stepfather breathes deep and steady.

It is harvest, the wheat golden in the fields all around;
the wind apple crisp.
Tomorrow, Jen reaches out to her daughter for a hug;
Mia, hesitant before an audience, returns to her mother.
Katie and I watch, holding hands.
The cows quiet as morning brightens
into warmth.

The god of lint

gathers softness from all the corners of a house,
collects the minute offerings
      of pets and storybook pages,
      teddy bears and pajamas,
      washcloths and comforters,
          all that has touched skin.

This god understands
          what it is to fray from stresses,
the friction points of knees on pants,
socks toe-worn running after errands
the daily grinding of bodies
      against their camouflages.

A god of repurposed particles forgives us
      our tatters and loose threads,
          patchwork relationships
      white lies and other shading,
          omissions and muzzy promises.

She/He/They—
      our trinity of bedroom and kitchen and living—
blends shed fibers into reincarnated clouds,
fading blues into gray,
      forests into sea foam,
          and reds into blushes.

Our household god of smallness and spreading
      needs our unraveling
          to make anew,
          knows to escape traps of our making
          and vent belonging across home
          in the breaking
             that we all breathe in.

Kami Nzeribe

She Is Everywhere

Crème blush. Apricot powder. A light application of blush. Liquid or crème blush is best applied before powder. "Pixie-dust." For this photo, dab on with your fingertips, glamour girl. Bee-stung lips. Natural lips. Blot more evenly. Blot your lips, again. Rub 'em together. Don't chew pink off revealing red or bright orange under. Continue, finishing touches: recurl your lashes, collect your points, pure honey. Re-apply and do it again. Make sure your lip pencil is sharpened to prevent lipstick from bleeding. Shimmer, Basquiat. Black mascara is applied to top lashes. Beige powder eyeshadow is powerful brushed on the brow bone. For oily complexions, use a highlighting "powder" to avoid a greasy look. Lashes, curled. Black mascara applied to top lashes only for a classical look. It does not have to be complicated to be classy. Classical application with a lip pencil is followed by two pleasurable applications of matte red lipstick. Pleasure yourself in beauty, in the time it takes, ingénue. Fire hid behind your teeth. Speak unique from powerful lips, sexy bitch. We paint a certain way, a different solar system of superstardom over here. Sensual. Modern-day Valentino. On your inner eye rim apply black eye pencil. Squeeze eyes shut, messy-looking mysterious highness. Take a round eyeshadow brush and blend in for a smokier atmospheric effect. Twirl in place; open starry eyes in surprise. Emphasize smile with a mid-neutral-toned lip pencil applied over entire lip. Bright colors used sparingly work best on Black skin to avoid looking chalky or ashy volcano. Then you curl all the lashes together and apply black mascara to top and bottom. Pay as much attention to bottom as the top and build equality. Build a new foundation by dusting rose blush on the cheeks. Release bright berry lip color with the lip brush, blotted, relined, then blotted again. Finish it off. Finish it with a lip moisturizer, Fun-Loving Spirit. This look can be worn by a person of any body, on any planet. Can slay, anybody can get it. Random temptress flesh-toned under frosted powder shadow swept over the entire eyelid, try using the rounded side of the sponge-tip applicator instead to help soften the "edge" of the black eye pencil along the outward and upward contours. Brush brows, Player One. Clear mascara, Heroine. Recurl them words, sweetie. Bear the striking likeness of a timeless statue, Icon. Bear it. Look boyish while remaining gamine. Shape it, Chanteuse. Curl up plumped lined lips painted Plum, Pam. Pull up, lion lady. Pose. Sing these moist lines with gloss applied to affix real mythic stature, you Diva. Stand down never, Madonna. Get beat to the bass. Sheer. Creamy. Glossy. Metallic. Face? Down. Taste it. She is Everywhere!

08: OVERRIPE

Stephanie Barbé Hammer

The Tired Magician

The magician was tired. His rabbit was tired, and his tall black hat was tired. The doves were tired of being crushed into tight spaces, and the playing cards were tired of disappearing and reappearing into wallets and shirt pockets. Even the famous saw that cuts the woman in half was so tired that it didn't notice that the woman involved in the illusion had become sick to death of squeezing her nether portions into that same constricting trick box. She refused this one time, and yet the saw did its usual work despite this new and surprising decision. So, chop chop went the saw, at which point the now liberated legs and lower torso of the female performer took to their heels and ran off-stage, leaving the top half to fend for itself, much to the discomfort of the audience in the little theater in the small but sophisticated west coast American city.

After some very restrained applause, the audience filtered out.

"I didn't know it was going to be that kind of performance," members of the city's New Residents Association Club said to each other. The words "avant-garde" and "grand guignol" were muttered as most people left and drowned their disappointment in the swank bars that surrounded the little theater.

The saw handed in its notice immediately after that disquieting performance, vowing to retire to a town that had the word "carpenter" in it, because the name was soothing, and reminded the saw of smooth shelves and cabinets. The top half of the woman also quit, but since she had lost her ambulatory section, she had herself carried off by four doves, who – if birds can look disdainfully at a person – did so to the magician, fluttering away from the stage, and out the door reserved for artists.

In this way, key elements of the magician's act came to be lost. Now, only two doves remained, as well as the enervated rabbit, an incomplete deck of exhausted cards, and the stalwart if somewhat battered hat.

The theater manager gave the magician to understand that he should not expect to be invited back any time soon.

The magician drove his old car home to his tall yet tiny apartment. You see, his studio was one of several eccentric floorplans that the city's famous architect designed so that it was actually 5 tiny floors and you had to walk upstairs to change spaces; kitchen on the ground floor, toilet, sink and shower on the top. In between, each on a separate floor: living, dining, and sleeping. There were no doors. Just stairs.

The apartment was lovely in a way, because when you came home you were always ascending. But it was so narrow that the magician felt a bit like Rapunzel in her tower, only the witch imprisoning him was not a person, but rather a quartette of financial institutions wishing to be paid. And these were not imprisoning him, but rather the opposite. The DMV, the IRS, the electric company, and the building management firm were constantly threatening to invade and throw him out – with ominous letters and knocks on the door – which necessitated a very long descent down to get the mail and explain to the particular power that was that he was doing his best and would explain more of his situation at length in a letter.

The magician's letters to these entities elucidated that he didn't make a lot of money to begin with and without the theater gig, he was currently a quite poor magician doing parties for the wealthy in the neighborhoods down the freeway near the polo fields. In addition he explained, people don't tend to tip a magician, so the magician made a flat flee with his cards, remaining doves and rabbit tricks, sometimes doing close magic where he made people's watches and handkerchiefs disappear, but people don't get as excited about all that as they used to.

After he took the letters to the post office, he came back to the apartment, climbed up to the roof, considered his situation and did the one thing he could think to do. Which was to go all the way back down to the kitchen and bake some blueberry muffins to cheer himself up. Because, there's nothing like a snack. As he preheated the oven and poured the batter into the little cups, he wondered if he should get an advanced degree of some kind; perhaps he should become -- instead of a magician -- an actual wizard, which might have some cachet and enhanced professional opportunities.

Yes! More education must be the answer!

That night he considered visiting the local wizard college, and making inquiries about applying there. But an internet search revealed that the physical premises of the college were hard to locate. Reddit and Quora informed him that the college could be glimpsed outside of taverns and on the edge of a golf course but would often vanish as soon as you approached it. Which made sense. Of course, a wizard college would be had to find, because you have to keep out the riff raff -- those who might visit the college on a lark but are not truly enthusiastic and passionate about the wizarding field.

But one day, the magician received some unexpected assistance. He was parking the car after an underpaid performance at a retirement banquet (where, due to a slight inaccuracy, he had made the honoree disappear and then reappear, in a semi-recumbent position right in the middle of a large and sticky upside-down cake), when he noticed a woman in large sunglasses, an elegant suede coat and bedroom slippers. From the slippers he guessed she might be houseless. But he felt somehow that she knew things, perhaps from the authoritative way that she went through the dumpster, flinging things into recycling, or more rarely inserting something into her coat pockets and shopping bag.

He decided to follow the woman, just as she was rounding the corner and trailed her at a distance as she walked past the deli and the church to a park. He lost track of her amongst the trees. Then he noticed a little girl speaking emphatically to the turtles in a large pond, who were nodding their heads in agreement. Aha! A possible wizard! The magician approached but then halted; he hesitated to address an unaccompanied child. Happily an adult man – clearly the father -- materialized beside the youngster.

"Are either of you wizards?" he asked the pair.

"Almost," said the father. "We came close to getting our wizarding certificates, but then we dropped out, because we couldn't get through the 6-hour capstone exam."

"6 hours?" said the magician.

"Indeed," said the father. "I just couldn't manage the foreign language section or the essay section, so I walked out."

"And I quit in solidarity with my dad," the little girl piped up in that fiercely quiet voice that only the very young have.

The father looked fondly at his child. "She's a wonderful person, and arguably kindness and loyalty are more important than expertise."

The turtles nodded sagely.

The magician thanked them, and walked back to his tower apartment, feeling more tired than ever. 6 hours? He climbed up the stairs of his apartment. He stood on the roof. No answer came to him. He released the remaining doves and walked back down with his one rabbit. When the leasing office manager came by and pounded on the door, he gave the rabbit to her for her son, promising to pay up soon.

He looked at his old car and drove it to the train station, thinking he would just give up and become a hobo.

He stood for a moment, admiring the handsome old train station.

A large group was waiting for the train to the big city far away.

"I can't believe there's no place to get something to eat here," said a teenager to his companion.

"There isn't even a vending machine!" said the other mournfully.

The magician looked around. He noticed that, indeed, there was no snack bar at or next to the train station. No place to get a cup of coffee or a hot dog or a brownie. Everyone waiting for the train had what Shakespeare once called "a lean and hungry look."

The magician had an idea.

He drove home and baked some muffins. The next day he traded his car for a van. Then he brought his muffins and some plain old coffee in a thermos to the station. He opened the back of his van and offered the refreshments to people for a low price and people bought them. A week went by. Two. He paid the rent. He paid the DMV. He got a bigger coffee maker and offered more coffee. Sometimes he did a magic trick or two, while the coffee was brewing. Some customers did, in fact, tip. He juggled the coins, and they glinted in sunlight or lamplight before disappearing one, two, three, into his pockets. Sometimes one would appear, behind a child's ear. An ancient manoeuver, but one that always delighted.

This magician's new business was not a big thing. He didn't make a lot more money but he made enough, for the moment, and the selling of the snacks gave him satisfaction so that when he climbed the stairs to his narrow apartment on 5 different floors, he felt more content than he had in a long time. He brewed his own cup of coffee and went all the way up and stood on the roof. Below him the woman in the suede coat and sunglasses went through the garbage, so he walked down and out and offered her a cup. She took it, gesturing silently that while coffee was not her preferred beverage, she appreciated the offer.

The magician nodded appreciatively, as the woman drained her cup, gave it back to him, whipped off her glasses and opened her coat. The magician immediately recognized that this was his erstwhile assistant, the two halves of her torso neatly joined together with a red thread that perfectly matched her crimson two-piece bathing suit. The assistant pulled from her pocket two somewhat rumpled but still breathing doves. Then she smiled, revealing the Ace of Hearts clenched expertly in set of surprisingly white and healthy teeth.

Kim Dower

Why It's Important to Kill Ants

As I slam a paper towel over the stream of ants parading on my kitchen window sill, I think of Buddhists who'd tell me these sentient beings should not be harmed. I wonder, too, as I press my finger over the last one twitching, if I might be murdering my third grade teacher who looked a lot like an ant and who made us write a report on insects. Reincarnation is not as simple as coming back a cute white kitten. You don't get to choose your next life. The Buddhists say human beings are born and reborn an infinite number of times until they achieve Nirvana. It's looking very good that I'll be back, but hopefully not as an ant. Before I check out of this world I'll pray that I can return as an apricot teacup poodle, so someone beautiful can carry me in a Gucci tote, feed me treats on overnight flights to Bali, let me curl up on her belly while she sleeps. Dogs, no matter what size, don't give a shit about ants, but if ants crawl into a dog's kibble, the dog won't eat it, even though they provide vitamin C and protein. As nutritious as ants might be, dogs aren't stupid and they don't want anything crawling in their food. If I come back as a teacup poodle and I see ants in my gold plated dish I'd throw up for sure. I once heard about a baby rushed to the hospital because an ant crawled into her ear. This is a very compelling reason to kill ants on sight. In conclusion, unless you're a Buddhist or tell people you're a Buddhist, or if you simply believe in reincarnation, killing ants, when you see them in your home, even though they are only looking for water or a little bit of food, they protect our ecosystem, and are very social creatures, is the right move. Eliminate them before they take over.

How to Celebrate the End of the World

Undress.
Take everything off. Everything.
Rub your nipples with grape seed oil.
Sit up straight in your most uncomfortable chair.
Remind yourself of all the good things you've done.
Have you done anything good?
Tell me what you've done.
Have you given birth to a child
Who danced around the house wearing ninja clothes?
Did you visit your dying mother every last day until
The day she died whispering thank you inside your moist hands?
Be quiet.
Don't look me in the eyes. Look down.
Have you cooked meals for the homeless?
Sat with them while they ate?
Have you ever rescued anyone?
Tell me the good things you've done.
Then remember the times you lost yourself in sorrow.
Waded in pools of it, banged your head against the ledge,
Hated yourself for wanting love, or showing how you felt.
Remember the moments it hurt so bad you had to pull out
Just in time. Let's prepare together for the end of the world.
Forget what I previously said. Let's dress. Let's layer ourselves
With color, texture, linen and cashmere, beads in our hair, smear
Our blood on one another's faces. stretch ourselves
Into eternity, breathe life into whatever dream we've been keeping
Under wraps, jump the fence together, melt the line with heat
From our kisses, obliterate it with desire, cross over
Into the end of the world, the beginning of another, locked
In an emergency embrace.

Rob Kunz

A Soul's Descent Two Ways

09: REUNITE

Janet McMillan Rives

Grafted

a supple body at home
among lofty branches
a young child
a climber   a scrambler

over time   a self
ripped apart   thin skin
bruises   replacement parts
that don't fit well

an entire vocabulary
from another language
words of   anatomy
of   physiology

unhinged
by artificial   movements
detachments
misunderstandings

till finally   parts mesh
form a composite
grafted from change
connection   memory

the view again
from high in the maple
the whole of life
laid out below

Kareem Tayyar

The Queen of Snow

My favorite film of my grandmother's is one that almost no one remembers. Released in 1928—and the last of the thirty-seven silents she starred in during the decade—The Queen of Snow concerns an old woman whom, disoriented as a result of her failing memory, exits her Northeastern cottage on the second day of a blizzard and, after accidentally wandering out onto a frozen lake, slips through the ice into the frigid water below. However, as she begins to sink towards the bottom, a mermaid (never mind that we are in freshwater) swims towards her, wraps her arms around the old woman's shoulders, and begins to guide the two of them towards what appears to be a castle whose walls and turrets are comprised of ice, and whose drawbridge is made from the hood of a repurposed Ford Roadster. Once inside, the two are almost immediately surrounded by several other mermaids, the most striking of whom approaches the old woman, places her lips to the old woman's lips, and breathes life into the old woman that not only immediately revives her, but that shaves several decades off her proverbial odometer. Soon enough the formerly-old-but-now-young woman is delivered by her rescuer back onto solid ground, where she will spend the rest of the movie attempting to figure out what to do with a life that she is, most unexpectedly, able to live again.

My grandmother, the famous actress Annie Bloom, played the main character, and even though she would give more storied performances in vastly more highly-regarded pictures, The Queen of Snow remains the movie of hers that I return to most often. Why this is I'm not certain, though I'm sure part of it has to do with the simple fact that it was the first movie of hers that I ever saw.

Which means that I cannot remember a time in my life when my grandmother didn't seem to exist in rather close proximity to the fantastical.

Which also means that when I received a call in the autumn of 1981 that she had disappeared from the Hollywood Legacy Retirement Home, my first, admittedly ridiculous, thought was that she'd decided to return to some underwater kingdom within the Los Angeles city limits that only she was aware existed.

Of course, that isn't what happened.

Not exactly, anyway.

The retirement home was located high above Sunset Boulevard, situated on a bluff that afforded a panoramic view of the city that could easily trick the viewer into thinking Los Angeles was still a beautiful place. A fitting dynamic for a facility that housed retired creatives whose professional lives had been devoted, to paraphrase the final lines of The Man Who Shot Liberty Valance, to "printing the legend instead of the truth."

Upon entering the sprawling lobby—in the middle of which was a fountain dominated by a larger-than-life sculpture of Errol Flynn as Robin Hood—I was immediately met by Hollywood Legacy's two, for lack of a better word, proprietors: the general manager (a man named Asher who wore an impeccably pressed and tailored pinstripe suit) and the head doctor, whose name I can no longer recall.

After the initial handshakes they quickly ushered me through a series of familiar hallways and elevators and into my grandmother's fourth-floor room. Given that I was a regular visitor to the establishment, the men knew that a basic overview of the layout and operations of the facility were not required, and therefore our walk was done in silence.

However, upon entering my grandmother's room—which she'd decorated, as she had every place she'd ever lived, with a Jazz Age sensibility that included colored scarves draped over the lampshades, a few original Toulouse Lautrec paintings on the walls, and a number of Fitzgerald, Hemingway, and John O'Hara first editions on the coffee table she'd always insisted Douglas Fairbanks had made especially for her—the general manager immediately said,

"First, we'd like to offer our apologies for what has happened. It is unacceptable and, in addition to having alerted the police, a number of our off-duty nurses and employees are out scouring the area for her as we speak."

Before I could either accept or refuse his apology, the doctor, who seemed the type that would ask a gunshot victim in the process of bleeding out to sign a number of forms exempting the doctor from possible malpractice claims before providing treatment, added,

"Of course, our residents are not inmates, meaning they are free to come and go as they please."

Vietnam had been full of men like the doctor, ex-ROTC cadets from Ivy League institutions whom, not having had the courage to head for Canada and save the rest of us from their sanctimony, spent their tours treating those in their charge like personal courtiers rather than fellow countrymen.

In other words, had the circumstances been different, it's likely I would have spent several minutes engaged in the kind of senseless, angry back-and-forth I so often did in those years, when I used almost any opportunity I could to re-litigate the wrongs I felt that I—and so many others—had experienced as a result of the decisions men like this doctor had made.

But in a rare moment of restraint, I simply responded,

"I'd like to speak to your colleague alone for a few moments."

The doctor, clearly surprised, and not a little insulted, took a few moments to absorb my request before responding.

"Of course."

Upon his exit, I turned to the general manager and said,

"When was she last seen?"

"The nurse on duty tried to deliver her dinner at 4:00 p.m."

"Tried?" I asked, while through the large bay windows I noticed two nurses in white uniforms helping an old man in a wheelchair—and whom I recognized as a former character actor who'd made a career playing heavies and toughs—fly a kite that was shaped like a small giraffe.

"Apparently Annie didn't care for the way the steak had been cooked, nor did she care for the cheese-fries that came with it."

"I'm sure she didn't," I said.

The general manager, whom I'd prepared myself to dislike, but whom instead seemed a warm- hearted fellow whose understated demeanor failed to mask a clear concern for his residents, smiled as well.

"Your grandmother takes her food very seriously," he said.

"She does indeed," I added.

We stood in several seconds of the kind of silence that exists between two men who want to laugh but know, given the circumstances, they shouldn't, before I said,

"Is the nurse who last saw her still on duty?"

"Yes."

"I'd like to speak with her."

"Of course. One moment."

He slipped quietly out of the bedroom, and in the minute or two that I was alone, I crossed to the window and watched the kite floating back and forth across the cloudless sky. Not, I should mention, because I found it soothing, nor because it reminded me of some childhood memory tied to my grandmother. After all, if my grandmother could be said to possess any inclination towards the playful in her life, it was in her willingness to fully commit to whatever role she was portraying on screen, be it cabaret dancer (The Moon Wore High Heels), hopeless romantic (Another Wish for the Road), circus performer (Under the Big Top), sharp-shooter (The Second Coming of Annie Oakley), or fortune-teller (I'll Tell You Tomorrow).

Rather, I think the reason I can still remember the image of that giraffe-shaped kite all these years later is because it may have been the first time in the decade since I'd returned stateside that the idea of doing something just for the hell of it had ever occurred to me.

Soon enough, however, the door opened behind me, and the general manager and the nurse—one of my grandmother's favorites, a forty-something woman named Dorothy whose near-religious devotion to the movies meant the two of them were always arguing about the relative merits of a particular film—entered.

"I'm so sorry about this, Charlie," Dorothy said.

"There's nothing to apologize for," I answered. "We both know Annie. I'm surprised something like this hadn't happened sooner."

"Did she say anything else that struck you as unusual when you spoke to her earlier today?" I continued, suddenly aware I was beginning to sound perilously close to the type of detective featured in the noir pictures my grandmother hated.

"Nothing," Dorothy answered. "She just said she was done eating prison food, and that the minute she got the chance she was going to have herself a real meal."

"A real meal?"

Dorothy shrugged.

"That's what she said. A real meal. Fettuccine Alfredo, white burgundy wine, and a large slice of chocolate cake."

I smiled.

"You can call off the dogs," I said. "I'll have her back in a few hours."

It was still early enough in the evening that Hollywood Boulevard wasn't the parking lot it would become a few hours later. Certainly the blocks were crowded with sunburned tourists taking photographs in front of the Egyptian Theater with costumed actors pretending to be Charlie Chaplin (whom my grandmother detested), Humphrey Bogart (whom she'd had an affair with), and Marilyn Monroe (ditto), but traffic was relatively smooth, and I made it to Musso and Frank's, an establishment which, even by 1981, was the oldest-surviving restaurant in the City of Angels, shortly before 6 p.m.

It's impossible to say how often she had taken me there when I was a child, but each time we'd
sit in the corner booth where she'd first signed a contract with the fledgling Paramount Studios. No matter the occasion: my first Little League home run, my first heartbreak, my last night as a free man before shipping off to boot camp, Musso's was where the two of us would go, and where she would, without fail, order the Fettuccine Alfredo, a glass of white burgundy wine, and a large slice of chocolate cake. Among her many other qualities, the woman remained, until the last days of her long life, a creature of habit par excellence.

After pulling into the parking lot behind the restaurant, entering through the back entrance, and walking past the bank of wooden phone booths that lined the hallway separating one of the two dining areas from the restrooms, I approached the host's stand, which on that particular evening was inhabited by a woman in her early sixties whose long, silver hair gave her an almost mystic beauty, and said,

"I'm here to meet Annie Bloom."

"Right this way, sir," the woman said. "She'd mentioned someone would be joining her."

I followed her into the larger of the two dining areas, along whose far left wall was a bar famous for its dry martinis, and soon arrived in front of our regular booth. The hostess quietly slipped out of the frame, and once she was out of earshot and my grandmother and I had spent a good five or six seconds looking at one another, she was the first to break the silence.

"What took you so long? I'm starving."

I slid into the booth across from her, whose high-backed red vinyl gave her the look of an imperious queen in exile, and said,

"Why do you always make things so difficult?"

"Jack Warner once asked me the same question."

"Yeah? And what did you say."

"Because I'm worth it."

"I'm not sure about that. The films you made for Warner Brothers were terrible."

"What about The Last Starlet?"

"You must be joking."

"Once Upon an Autumn?"

"I won't even dignify that one with a response."

"Yesterday is Already Tomorrow?"

"Now you're just being silly."

"You always were a tough crowd."

"And you always had a soft spot for terrible scripts."

"You haven't given me a kiss yet."

"I'm not sure you deserve one. You almost gave Asher a heart attack. Dorothy too."

"Then they should serve better food. I was starting to feel like William Holden in Bridge on the River Kwai."

"How did you get here, by the way?"

"I still know a few people in this town."

"None who haven't had their car keys taken away."
Our waiter, sporting the usual red jacket as well as a mustache that could have had its own area code, approached, and asked,

"What can I get you to drink?"

"I think we're ready to order, actually," I said.

"Wonderful. What would you like?"

When our plates had been cleared, and the wine had been drunk, and I'd paid the check and retrieved my
grandmother's wheelchair, the two of us exited the restaurant. It was nearly 9 p.m. and, rare for a Los
Angeles night, there were enough stars in the sky for us to locate the handful of constellations that both of us knew. After a few moments of stargazing, however, my grandmother's attention seemed to be on something across the street.

"What is it?" I asked, as I reached into my pocket to retrieve the valet ticket.

"I'm not sure," she said, already beginning to wheel herself in the direction of whatever it was she was looking at.

I gestured towards the valet, a young man in his early twenties whose blonde hair and deep tan signified one who would always, no matter the season, Rather Be Surfing, that we'd be right back, and I caught up to my grandmother and began pushing her chair.

As we moved towards the street I noticed it too. A large mural could be seen on an equally large wall in the alley on the other side of the street, painted in bright turquoises and blues which were illuminated by the several lights that shone from the roof of a nearby building. There were scenes like it all over the city in those days— and probably today, as well, though I moved out of L.A. years ago and have never returned—where mostly anonymous artists turned the sides of old warehouses, supermarkets, and clothing stores into sprawling canvases upon which to work.

Having crossed the street and wheeled her into a position where we could take in the entirety of the image, what we saw was an undersea world filled with winged seahorses, fluorescent shells, buried treasure, shimmering grass, and, in the left-hand panel of the mural, two mermaids, one young, one old, their tails curled around each other's, and both looking up towards a moon that somehow shone above them, even though they must have been miles beneath the surface of the ocean.

Neither of us spoke for several minutes. And though the noises of the city went on around us— the whirring blades of a police helicopter, the voices of drunks arguing over the Dodgers, the blaring of an ambulance siren, the honking of horns and the shrieks of local revelers—it didn't diminish the feeling that we'd stumbled onto holy land, and that therefore the only appropriate response was to remain in reverent silence for as long as we possibly could.

Then, finally, my grandmother reached back, took my hand, and said,

"Alright. I'm ready."

Robb Kunz

Color Story First Band

As Far as Pieces Missing

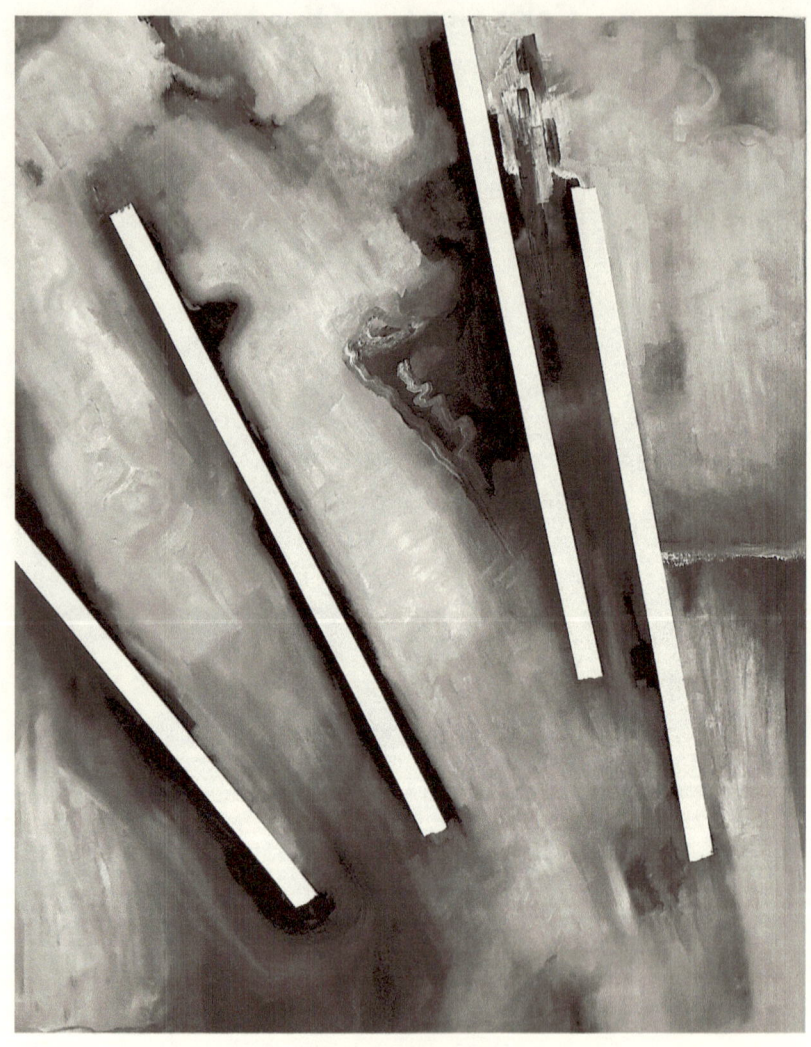

Gaia in Tree Form

Into Black and White

Leafless

Nancy Issenman

Reincarnation: Notes to Self

Cut the cord gently but close.
Make sure your skin fits this time.

Cry a lot those first days, then settle
into quiet grief, one that knows itself
as a cold layer of mid-winter snow.

Clean the clutter left behind.
Leave your walls bare for a time.
Taste before you swallow,
even go hungry.

Practice everything. Violin arpeggios,
silence, kindness. Breathing.

Run away often but keep your soul nearby.
Don't become lost in smoky rooms
where you trade virtue for fugitive thrills.

Come back as a Jew again, despite
betrayals, despite everything.
This time gather the wisdom knotted
in the Rabbi's tattered *tallis*.

Listen. What the elders say matters.
Become familiar with broken chords.
Begin again with *repair of the world*.

Bring back the ghost box: small bones
of a hummingbird, papyrus, star dust,
scratched missives on polar ice,
• the murmur of fallen trees.

Feast on words. They call you back.

Recall that everything we love,
we lose.

Diane Douiyssi

to soar

the orange, sweet
   word blooms
      on your
       tongue as
          if it's a
           slice of
             mandarin,
           a gold
                 droplet,
   a melt of
     sweet chocolate

         you lift it
           tender,
           cup the
           word and
          place it
          on the page
            where it
            swells with
              the clementine
             wings of
             butterflies,
          shimmering
           sands of a
           desert that
              hover above you

you release
        it
        kissing it with
            a soft
                breath of
                longing
            before it
                                lifts
        from the open page
        to make its
            way into
                the wind, to
    find the spiral ear
    of another's
            heart

listen—
    a joy, a sorrow,
    a permission opens
its wet wings
    and you
            stand still—
        watch it
                    soar

About the Contributors

Nancy Beagle finds poetry to be pilgrimage, an ongoing journey toward truth and understanding. Her life has been spent as a creative artist—as songwriter, musician, actress, playwright, and poet. While majoring in music at USC, she was mentored by poet Mark McCloskey and later earned her doctorate in Early Music from Stanford University. She has performed her music and plays throughout California, performing at the Huntington Library as well as at many universities and clubs and has received several awards for her work as an actress and teacher, including National Endowment and Fulbright grants.

Patricia Behrens lives in New York City. Her poetry has appeared in publications such as *Crab Orchard Review, Split Rock Review, The Literary Bohemian, The Road Not Taken, Think, American Arts Quarterly* and *Nasty Women Poets: An Unapologetic Anthology of Subversive Verse.*

Chanel Brenner is the winner of the 2021 Press 53 Award for *Poetry for Smile, or Else.* She is the author of *Vanilla Milk: a memoir told in poems,* (Silver Birch Press, 2014), which was a finalist for the 2016 Independent Book Awards and honorable mention in the 2014 Eric Hoffer awards. Her work has appeared in *The Rumpus, Tahoma Literary Review, HerStry, Modern Loss, The Good Men Project, New Ohio Review, Poet Lore, Rattle, Barrow Street, Salamander, Spoon River Poetry Review, Literary Mama,* and others. Her poem, "July 28th" won first prize in The Write Place at the Write Time's contest, judged by Ellen Bass, and her poem, "Apology," won first place in the Smartish Pace Beullah Rose Poetry Prize.

Shirley J. Brewer (Baltimore, MD) serves as poet-in-residence at Carver Center for the Arts, and on the board of directors of Passager Books. Shirley's poems garnish *The Comstock Review, Poetry East, Paterson Literary Review, Spillway, Tar River Poetry,* and many other journals and anthologies. Her books include *A Little Breast Music* (Passager Books), *After Words* (Apprentice House), *Bistro in Another Realm* (Main Street Rag), and *Wild Girls* (Apprentice House). Shirley's poems are part of the Lunar Codex program and are currently on the moon! Website: www.shirleyjbrewer.com.

Joanne Clarkson's sixth poetry collection, *Hospice House*, was released by MoonPath Press in 2023. Her volume, *The Fates*, won Bright Hill Press' annual contest and appeared in 2017. Her poems have been published in such journals as *Poetry Northwest, Nimrod, Poet Lore, Alaska Quarterly Review* and *American Journal of Nursing*. Clarkson has Masters Degrees in English and Library Science, has taught and worked for many years as a professional librarian. After caring for her mother through a long illness, she re-careered as a Hospice RN. See more at www.joanneclarkson.com.

Patricia Davis-Muffett (she/her) holds an MFA from the University of Minnesota. Her chapbook, *Alchemy of Yeast and Tears*, was published in spring 2023. Her work has won honors including the 2023 Erskine J Poetry Prize, Best of the Net nomination, second place in the 2024 Joe Gouveia Outermost Poetry Contest (selected by Marge Piercy) and appears in *Best New Poets, Smartish Pace, Atlanta Review, Calyx and About Place*, among others.

Peggy Dobreer is a four-time Pushcart nominated poet with two collections titled *In the Lake of Your Bones* and *Drop and Dazzle* both from Moon Tide Press. She has written reviews for *Poetry Flash*, taught in Red Hen's WITS Program, was a Program Director at AROHO 2015 and has received fellowships from Community of Writers, The Institute for the Study of Los Angeles, and The School of Anglophile Studies at Charles University in Prague. She is the curator and Editor of Slow Lightning Lit, a tiny new L.A. indie press. www.slowlightninglit.com.

Kim Dower was City Poet Laureate of West Hollywood from 2016 – 2018. Author of five collections of poetry: *Air Kissing on Mars*, "sensual and evocative . . . seamlessly combining humor and heartache," (Los Angeles Times), *Slice of Moon*, "unexpected and sublime," ("O" Magazine), *Last Train to the Missing Planet*, "poems that speak about the grey space between tragedy and tenderness, memory and loss, fragility and perseverance," (Inaugural Poet, Richard Blanco), the Gold Ippy Award winning, *Sunbathing on Tyrone Power's Grave*, and her latest, *I Wore This Dress Today for You, Mom*, "A fantastic collection." (Washington Post). Dower's poems have been featured on Garrison Keillor's "The Writer's Almanac" as well as in many journals and anthologies. She teaches poetry workshops for UCLA Extension, and the West Hollywood Library. Her next collection, *What She Wants*: *Poems on Obsession, Desire, Despair, Euphoria* was published by Red Hen Press in January, 2025. www.kimdowerpoetry.com

Nathaniel Dolton-Thornton's poems are published or forthcoming in *Tin House, Vallum, Griffith Review, Gulf Coast, Sugar House Review, Lake Effect, Magma Poetry, Sixth Finch, Poetry Salzburg Review, Salamander, Sycamore Review, TAB, The Account, Constellations, Tipton Poetry Journal, Raritan, Hampden-Sydney Poetry Review, Tupelo Quarterly*, and other publications.

Brian Duran-Fuentes was born and raised in Mexico City. His work has appeared in several publications including *Oyez Review, Ravens Quoth Press, Thimble Literary Magazine, Paladín Magazine, Hyperbole Frontera, Irradiación, Digo.Palabra.TXT* and *Voicemail Poems*. He holds a bachelor's degree in English, Spanish, and Translation-Interpreting from the University of Texas at Arlington and a master's degree in Creative Writing from the University of Salamanca. His most recent book Sleep Studies at the Mercy of Kaiju is out on Ukiyoto Press.

Diane Roberson Douiyssi is a poet and writer currently living near the earth and peoples that nourish the world in South Dakota in the United States. She's a lifelong writer who received her B.A. from Grinnell College. Her poems have appeared or will soon appear in *Amethyst Review, Pasque Petals, song of ourself,* and *World Lives, Prairie Living*. She's founder of Inner Wisdom Wayfinding, where she hosts writing workshops and mentors women who want to tell their stories.

Kami Enzie (he/him), a Vienna-born, New Orleans-raised queer Nigerian-Filipino writer, is a recent Iowa MFA grad. His work appears, or will soon, in *Black Warrior Review, Chicago Review, fourteen poems, The Glacier, Image, The Journal, Ki, Obsidian, Oversound, The Poetry Review, swamp pink*, and elsewhere. He is an alumnus of Tin House Winter Workshops, VCFA's Postgraduate Writers' Conference, and 2024 winner of the poetry contest for the Tennessee Williams & New Orleans Literary Festival. IG/X: @yungwerther.

Poet/photographer **Alexis Rhone Fancher** is published in *Best American Poetry, Rattle, The American Journal of Poetry, Spillway, Plume, Diode, The Pedestal Magazine*, and elsewhere. She's authored ten poetry collections, most recently, *TRIGGERED*, (MacQueens) and *BRAZEN* (NYQ). A coffee table book of Alexis' photographs of Southern California poets will be published by Moon Tide Press in 2026. She calls the Mojave Desert home.

Michael J. Galko is a scientist and poet who lives and works in Houston, TX. He was a 2019 Pushcart Award nominee, a finalist in the 2020 Naugatuck River Review narrative poetry contest, and a finalist in the 2022 Bellevue Literary Review poetry contest. In the past year he has had poems published or accepted at *North Dakota Quarterly, Noon: journal of the short poem, Eclectica, Clackamas Literary Journal, Tar River Poetry*, and *Cordite Poetry Review*, among other journals.

Edward Santos Garza is a photographer and writer based in Houston. His photos have been published by *SB Nation, *Infrarrealista Review**, and the *Latino Cultural Center in Dallas*, among other venues. Follow him on Instagram @EdwardSGarza.

Therese Gleason's poetry, flash fiction, essays, and hybrid work have appeared in *32 Poems, Atticus Review, Cincinnati Review, Indiana Review, Lunch Ticket, New Ohio Review, On the Seawall, Rattle*, and elsewhere. She is author of three chapbooks: *Hemicrania* (forthcoming, Chestnut Review, 2024), about living with chronic migraine; *Matrilineal* (Finishing Line, 2021); and *Libation* (co-winner, 2006 South Carolina Poetry Initiative Competition). Originally from Louisville, Kentucky, she currently lives with her family in central Massachusetts, where she teaches English language and literacy to multilingual learners in the Worcester Public Schools. www.theresegleason.com

Stephanie Barbe Hammer is a 7-time Pushcart Prize nominee in fiction, nonfiction and poetry. Her work appears in a bunch of places including the *Chiron Review, Pearl, Hayden's Ferry* and *Phantom Drift*. Her most recent novel Journey to Merveilleux City is a finalist for the Foreword INDIE award, mystery category. She is a professor emerita at UC Riverside and teaches writing for the Inlandia Institute and the Santa Barbara Writers Conference. She lives in Santa Barbara with her husband, writer Larry Behrendt.

Susan Hayden is the author of *Now You Are a Missing Person*, a lyrical memoir in poems, stories and fragments (Moon Tide Press, 2023). The book received the Kirkus Star from Kirkus Reviews, was an Eric Hoffer Book Award Finalist, a Zibby Awards Finalist, an NIEA Awards Finalist, included in LA Public Library's Best of 2023/ Literature and Fiction and shortlisted for The Memoir Prize for Books. It was also named Winner in both Poetry and Wild Card categories by the Southern California Book Festival. She has contributed to numerous anthologies, including From *Venice to Venice* (El Martillo Press), *Beat Not Beat* (Moon Tide Press), *Los Angeles in the 1970s* (Rare Bird Books) and *The Black Body* (Seven Stories Press). Hayden is the creator/producer of Library Girl, a monthly literary series now in its 16th year at Ruskin Theatre.

Lesley Roger Hobbs (she/her) is an Irish poet and artist living in the Pacific Northwest with her husband and dog. She is inspired by nature, long walks and all things Celtic, she loves popcorn, sunshine, Pink Floyd and the ocean. Her poetry has appeared in *Open Door Poetry, The Hyacinth Review, Querencia Press* and *Cirque*.

Trish Holden teaches environmental science and management and writes poetry about major life reflections that occur with age. Poetry is her preferred creative outlet for emotion, a destination for making meaning of observations and associated strong feelings. She likes that her poems can carry a certain and breathlessness, at once. Her style is either to write with impact in short form, or to write in a longer form that edges towards narrative and recounts an intense interaction.

LeAnne Hunt (she/her) is a Pushcart-nominated poet now living in Mississippi. She edits manuscripts for Arroyo Seco Press and has poems published in *Cultural Weekly, Spillway, Hybrid Harpy Review* and *Lullaby of Teeth: An Anthology of Southern California Poets*. She publishes a blog of writing prompts and apologies at www.leannehunt.com.

J.D. Isip's collections include *Reluctant Prophets* (Moon Tide Press, 2025), *Kissing the Wound* (Moon Tide Press, 2023), and *Pocketing Feathers* (Sadie Girl Press, 2015). J.D. teaches in South Texas where he lives with his dogs, Ivy and Bucky.

Nancy Issenman, a Jewish, queer writer and artist, lives on unceded Lekwungen territory, aka Victoria, BC. Nancy has published a chapbook, *The Name of Yes*, and her poems have appeared in various publications including the anthology *The Sky is Falling, The Sky is Falling* (Goldfinch Press), *Lilac Arch Press, Sea and Cedar Magazine* and *Island Writers Magazine*. One of her stories was published in *don't tell: family secrets* (Demeter Press.) A plaque with one of her poems was recently installed in Alta Lake Park, Whistler BC, after winning the Whistler Poetry Pause prize, 2004.

Michael Juliani is a poet, editor, and writer from Pasadena, California. He graduated with a Print & Digital Journalism degree from the University of Southern California and a creative writing MFA in poetry from Columbia University. His poetry manuscript, *The World Is Not Astonished*, was named a finalist for the 2021 Jake Adam York Prize (Copper Nickel/Milkweed Editions) for a first or second collection of poetry. His articles, essays, interviews, poems, and stories have appeared in outlets such as the *Los Angeles Times, Los Angeles Review of Books, BOMB, Epiphany, Guernica, Bennington Review, Sixth Finch*, and the *Washington Square Review*. He lives in Los Angeles.

Ron Koertge writes a lot about a lot of things. Visit my website if you want to know more.

Robb Kunz hails from Teton Valley, Idaho. He received his MFA in creative writing from the University of Idaho. He currently teaches writing at Utah State University and is the Art and Design Faculty Advisor of *Sink Hollow: An Undergraduate Literary Journal*. His art has been published in *Peatsmoke Journal, Red Ogre Review, Fatal Flaw Literary Magazine*, and *New Delta Review*. His art is upcoming in *Whisper and Roars, Glassworks Magazine*, and the *NonBinary Review*.

Amanda Le is a Vietnamese-American artist local to Southern California. They identify as a nonbinary artist and as a bisexual, and is proud to represent LGBTQ+ Artists in literature. They earned a BA in Art and a Masters in Education from UC Irvine. Amanda designed a BIBA Award-winning book cover for poetry anthology "A Burning Lake of Paper Suns" by Ellen Webre. Amanda became a full-time book illustrator in 2023. They are a lifelong lover of stories and art, and creates art that focuses on kindness and art as healing.

Gahl Liberzon is a writer and educator in Long Beach, California. His work has appeared in *The Museum of Americana* and *The Golden Shovel Anthology: New Poems Honoring Gwendolyn Brooks*, and he has previously taught and performed throughout southeast Michigan, the greater Chicago area, and the greater Tokyo Metropolitan area.

Yvette R. Murray is an award-winning poet and the author of *Hush, Puppy* (Finishing Line Press 2023). She has been published in *Chestnut Review, Aunt Chloe, Emrys Journal, Litmosphere, A Gathering Together*, and others. She is the 2022 Susan Laughter Meyers Weymouth Fellow, a 2021 Best New Poet selection, a Watering Hole Fellow, and a Pushcart Prize nominee. Find her on Twitter @MissYvettewrites or at Missyvettewrites@gmail.com.

Robbi Nester is a retired college educator who lives and writes in Southern California. She is the author of 4 books of poetry and editor of three anthologies and currently hosts two monthly poetry Zooms. Learn more at her website, www.robbinester.net.

Poet, essayist, translator, and Fulbright Scholar, **Rachel Neve Midbar's** collection *Salaam of Birds* (Tebot Bach 2020) was chosen by Dorothy Barresi for the Patricia Bibby First Book Prize. She is also the author of the chapbook, *What the Light Reveals* (Tebot Bach, 2014, winner of The Clockwork Prize). Her poems and essays have been published widely in journals and anthologies. She is the co-editor of *Stained: an anthology of writing about menstruation* (Querencia Press, July 2023) and the Editor in Chief of Calul Journal. More at www.rachelnevemidbar.com.

Terri Niccum's full-length collection, *The Knife Thrower's Daughter*, was released in 2022 from Moon Tide Press. She is also the author of the chapbooks *Dead Letter Box* (Moon Tide Press) and *Looking Snow in the Eye* (Finishing Line Press). Her upcoming chapbook from Moon Tide is *Sky Leaning Toward Winter*. Niccum was a finalist and runner-up for the 2020-2021 Steve Kowit Poetry Prize and a finalist for the Atlanta Review 2024 International Poetry Competition. Her work has appeared in *A Moon of One's Own*, an online journal from *Picture Show Press*; *Atlanta Review*; *Nimrod International Journal*; *Golden Streetcar*; *The Maine Review*; *Oberon Poetry*; and the *Pomona Valley Review*, among others.

Janet McMillan Rives lives in Oro Valley, Arizona. Her poems have appeared in such journals as *Beyond Words, Lyrical Iowa, Raw Art Review, Ekphrastic Review, MacQueen's Quinterly, Crosswinds, Creosote and Canary*. She is the author of three poetry chapbooks: *Into This Sea of Green: Poems from the Prairie* (Finishing Line Press, 2020), *Washed by a Summer Rain: Poems from the Desert* (Kelsay Books, 2023), and *On Horsebarn Hill: Poems* (Kelsay Books, 2024). Her hybrid memoir, *Thread: A Memoir in Woven Poems* (Finishing Line Press) was published in 2024.

Elaine Mintzer lives in Los Angeles. Her work has been published most recently in *Anacapa Review* and *Shiela-Na-Gig*. Her work has been featured on Moon Tide Press poet-of-the-month page, *Cultural Weekly, MacQueen's Quinterly, Beloit Poetry Review, Panoplyzine, Slipstream Press, Silver Birch Press, Gyroscope Review, Last Call, Chinaski*, and *Lummox*. Elaine's first collection was *Natural Selections* (Bombshelter Press 2005).

Todd Robinson has published two poetry collections, most recently *Mass for Shut-Ins* (University of Nebraska Press, 2018). His work has appeared or is forthcoming in *The Adroit Journal*, *North American Review*, and *Rattle*. He is an Assistant Professor in the Writer's Workshop at the University of Nebraska-Omaha and caregiver to his partner, a disabled physician. Learn more at www.toddfather.net

Lao Rubert lives in Durham, North Carolina. Her poems have appeared in *Adanna*, *Atlanta Review*, *Barzakh*, *Collateral*, *Mom Egg Review*, *Muleskinner*, *Poetry in Plain Sight*, *2024 Pinesong Award Anthology*, *Poetry East*, *Wordpeace* and elsewhere. Rubert received an M.A. in English Literature from Duke University and has spent a career working to reform the criminal justice system.

Alicia Vogl Saenz (she/ella) is a poet, meditation instructor, and museum professional at LACMA who brings her queer and mixed immigrant background to her writing and teaching. Vogl Saenz' parents met in Quito, Ecuador. Her mother, Ecuadorian, and her father given asylum in that country, from Czechoslovakia. She is deeply influenced by the expansive world view instilled from her parents. Her work has appeared in journals and anthologies such as *Grand Street*, *Blue Mesa Review*, *Mischief, Caprice*, and *Other Poetic Strategies* (Red Hen Press) and *Pratik*. She is the author of the chapbook *The Day I Wore the Red Coat* (VCP Press, 2001) and translated poet Mariano Zaro's book, *Tres Letras* (Walrus) into English. For the last 30 years, Alicia has performed her poetry throughout Southern California, most recently as part of the community celebrations of The Secret City. She is a member of Macondo Writers Workshop, the Lezarati Writer's Group, and has been in residence at Hedgebrook. Currently she is working on a manuscript inspired by Los Angeles as an ecosystem. Her blog, Translucent Matter can be found at www.aliciabird.me.

Marie Scarles is a writer, artist, and organizer from the marshlands of Mystic, CT, living and working in Brooklyn, NY. Her essays and poems have appeared in *The Believer*, *Los Angeles Review of Books*, *Tricycle Magazine*, *The Rumpus*, and elsewhere. By day, she works as the Communications Director at NY Renews, a climate and environmental justice coalition representing nearly 400 organizations across New York State. She earned her MFA in poetry and nonfiction from Rutgers University.

Aleksandra Scepanovic is a New York sculptor whose work explores the human condition through fragmented forms, celebrating wholeness amidst fracture and transformation. A former war reporter from the Balkans, she now lives and works between Woodstock and Brooklyn, NY, creating sculptures that embody themes of resilience, identity, and endurance.

Patricia L. Scruggs lives and writes in Southern California. In addition to her poetry collection, *Forget the Moon*, her work has appeared online and in print in *Burningword, ONTHEBUS, Spillway, RATTLE, Calyx, MacQueen's Quinterly, Crab Creek Review, Gyroscope Review, Inlandia* as well as the anthologies *13 Los Angeles Poets, So Luminous the Wildflowers, When Women Tell the Truth and Beyond the Lyric Moment*. A Pushcart Prize nominee, Patricia is a retired art educator who earned her MFA at California State University, Fullerton.

Amy Small-McKinney was the 2011 Montgomery County PA Poet Laureate. Her second full-length book, *Walking Toward Cranes*, won the Kithara Book Prize (Glass Lyre Press, 2017). Her chapbook, *One Day I Am a Field*, was written during COVID and her husband's death (Glass Lyre Press, 2022). Her poems have been published in the *American Poetry Review, The Baltimore Review, SWWIM, Tahoma Literary Review, Tiferet Journal, Literary Mama, Pedestal Magazine, Persimmon Tree*, and *Vox Populi*, among others. Her poems have also been translated into Korean and Romanian. Her third full-length book of poems *& You Think It Ends* is forthcoming 2025 (Glass Lyre Press).

Brian Sonia-Wallace is a writer in, and from, Los Angeles. Working across poetry, performance, and personal essay, they are interested in questions of self-expression, erasure, queerness, community, and commerce. They are a Harper Collins author, an Academy of American Poets Fellow, and the fourth Poet Laureate of the City of West Hollywood. Brian has been described the Department of Cultural Affairs as a "creative genius" and by *The New York Times* as "disappointingly normal."

Emily Tallman is a writer, songwriter and graphic designer living in Anchorage, AK. She toured nationally for nearly a decade and her music ranked for eight consecutive months on the Folk-DJ charts. Her poems have been published in *Catamaran Literary Reader*, *Cirque Journal* and *The Burden of Light: Poems on Illness and Loss*, among others. She has an MFA in Creative Writing from University of Alaska, Anchorage where she received the Jason Wenger Award for Excellence in Creative Writing.

Ben Trigg dreams of being Truly Outrageous, striving to be a safe space for all, but especially the queer community. He is one third of Two Idiots Peddling Poetry at the Ugly Mug in Orange, California, a weekly series that has been running since 2000. Ben's poetry has been described (by him) as the sweet spot junction of heartfelt, pop culture, and comedy. His collection *Kindness from a Dark God* came out on Moon Tide Press in 2007. He co-edited the anthology *Don't Blame the Ugly Mug: 10 Years of 2 Idiots Peddling Poetry*. When all else fails, Ben goes to Disneyland.

Rachel Walker is a poet from Maryland. She holds an MFA from the University of Nevada, Las Vegas, and is a doctoral student at the University of Missouri. Her work has recently appeared in *The Emerson Review*, *trampset*, *Lunch Ticket*, and *Hawai'i Pacific Review*.

Recipient of grants from the Whiting and Guggenheim foundations, **Charles Harper Webb's** latest collection of poems, *Sidebend World*, was published by the University of Pittsburgh Press. Red Hen Press published his novel *Ursula Lake* in Spring, 2022. His new collection of poems, *Old Gnu*, will be out from Longleaf Press in 2025.

Hilda Weiss is a poet and the co-founder/curator for www.poetry.la, a website featuring videos of poets and poetry venues in Southern California. Her poetry manuscript, *Seemingly Normal*, was awarded Honorable Mention by the National Federation of State Poetry Societies. She has a chapbook, *Optimism About Trees*, and has been published in *Spillway*, *Rattle*, *Tinderbox Poetry Journal*, *Cultural Weekly*, *Poemeleon*, and *Anti-Heroin Chic* among others. A fourth generation Californian, she lives, writes and grows her own vegetables in a garden full of native California plants in Santa Monica.

Dick Westheimer lives in rural southwest Ohio. He is winner of the 2023 Joy Harjo Poetry Prize and a Rattle Poetry Prize finalist. His poems have appeared or upcoming in *Only Poems, Whale Road Review, Rattle*, and *Minyan*. His chapbook, *A Sword in Both Hands, Poems Responding to Russia's War on Ukraine*, is published by SheilaNaGig.

Aruni Wijesinghe lives and writes in Southern California and can usually be found shelving books in the local public library. A project manager, ESL teacher, former sous chef and occasional belly dance instructor, she is a multiple Pushcart Prize and Best of the Net nominee. Her work has been published in *Spillway, Cultural Daily, Redshift, a moon of one's own, The Journal of Radical Wonder*, and elsewhere. She has multiple published collections including *2 Revere Place* (Moon Tide Press), *The Litany of Missing* and *Bedside Manners* (Arroyo Seco Press), and co-authored *The Undulating Line* (with Shannon Phillips and Suzanne Allen, Picture Show Press) and *God is a river running down my palm* (with Jeremy YS Ra, Picture Show Press). You can follow her on social media at @aruniwrites (Instagram and Twitter) or on her website www.aruniwrites.com.

Mariano Zaro is the author of six books of poetry: *Decoding Sparrows* (What Books, Los Angeles), *Padre Tierra* (Olifante, Zaragoza, Spain), Tres letras/Three Letters (Walrus, Barcelona), The House of Mae Rim/La casa de Mae Rim (Carayan Press, San Francisco), Poems of Erosion/Poemas de la erosión (Carayan Press, San Francisco) and Where From/Desde Donde (Bay Books). His poems have been included in the anthologies *Monster Verse* (Penguin Random House), *Wide Awake* (Beyond Baroque), *The Coiled Serpent* (Tía Chucha Press) and in several magazines in Spain, Mexico and the United States. His translations include *Poemas de las Misiones de California* by Philomene Long, *Buda en llamas* by Tony Barnstone and, in collaboration with Estíbaliz Espinosa and Amaia Gabantxo, *Cómo escribir una canción de amor* by Sholeh Wolpé. Zaro's short stories have appeared in *Portland Review, Pinyon, Baltimore Review, Louisville Review and Magnapoets*. He is the winner of the 2004 Roanoke Review Short Fiction Prize and the 2018 Martha's Vineyard Institute of Creative Writing Short Fiction Prize. Since 2010, he has been hosting a series of video-interviews with prominent American poets as part of the literary project Poetry.LA. Mariano Zaro earned a Ph.D. in Linguistics from the University of Granada (Spain) and a Master's in Literature from the University of Zaragoza (Spain). He is a professor of Spanish at Rio Hondo Community College (Whittier, California).

Jane Zich is a mixed media visual artist who explores imagery from the unconscious in her painting process. Her award-winning paintings have been exhibited nationally and featured on the covers of *American Psychologist, Dream Time, Fiction Fix, Jung Journal: Culture & Psyche,* and *Permafrost Magazine.* More of her artwork can be found at www.zichpaintings.com.

About the Guest Editors

Douglas Manuel was born in Anderson, Indiana and now resides in Long Beach, California. He received a BA in Creative Writing from Arizona State University, an MFA in poetry from Butler University, and a PhD in English Literature and Creative Writing from the University of Southern California. He is the author of two collections of poetry, Testify (2017) and Trouble Funk (2023). He is an assistant professor of English at Whittier College and teaches at Spalding University's low-res MFA program.

Steven Reigns is a Los Angeles poet and educator and was appointed the first Poet Laureate of West Hollywood. Alongside over a dozen chapbooks, he has published the collections Inheritance and Your Dead Body is My Welcome Mat. Reigns holds a BA in Creative Writing, a Master of Clinical Psychology, and is a seventeen-time recipient of The Los Angeles County's Department of Cultural Affairs' Artist in Residency Grant. He edited My Life is Poetry, showcasing his students' work from the first-ever autobiographical poetry workshop for LGBT seniors. Reigns has lectured and taught writing workshops around the country to LGBT youth and people living with HIV. Currently he is touring The Gay Rub, an exhibition of rubbings from LGBT landmarks, and is the board president of the Anaïs Nin Foundation. His collection A Quilt for David was published by City Lights and is the product of over ten years of research regarding dentist David Acer's life. His newest collection Outliving Michael is a memorial memoir in poetry, chronicling Reigns's profound friendship with Michael Church, who died of AIDS in 2000.

Notes and Acknowledgments

"Botanic Garden Built Over a Landfill" first appeared in the anthology *Women in a Golden State*, published by Gunpowder Press

"How to Celebrate the End of the World" appeared in *What She Wants" Poems on Obsession, Desire, Despair, Euphoria* (Red Hen Press, 2025)

"Homing" first appeared in *Underscore Magazine*

"I Don't Know How to Twist:" "A hustler is any woman in American Society" is a quote by author Studs Terkel from his book *Working*. The author also would like to note that some names in the essay have been changed for privacy.

"Poem Beginning with a Line from Richard Hugo" first appeared in the online journal *Loch Raven Review* (2022).

"The Myth of Magikarp" first appeared in *Honey Literary*.

Also Available from Moon Tide Press

Prayers With a Side of Cash, Kathleen Florence (2025)
Somewhere, a Playground, Rich Ferguson (2025)
The Tautology of Water, Giovanni Boskovich (2025)
Take Care, Mark Danowsky (2025)
Dilapitatia, Kelly Gray (2025)
Reluctant Prophets, J.D. Isip (2025)
Enormous Blue Umbrella, Donna Hilbert (2025)
Sky Leaning Toward Winter, Terri Niccum (2024)
Living the Sundown: A Caregiving Memoir, G. Murray Thomas (2024)
Figure Study, Kathryn de Lancellotti (2024)
Suffer for This: Love, Sex, Marriage, & Rock 'N' Roll,
    Victor D. Infante (2024)
What Blooms in the Dark, Emily J. Mundy (2024)
Fable, Bryn Wickerd (2024)
Diamond Bars 2, David A. Romero (2024)
Safe Handling, Rebecca Evans (2024)
More Jerkumstances: New & Selected Poems, Barbara Eknoian (2024)
Dissection Day, Ally McGregor (2023)
He's a Color Until He's Not, Christian Hanz Lozada (2023)
The Language of Fractions, Nicelle Davis (2023)
Paradise Anonymous, Oriana Ivy (2023)
Now You Are a Missing Person, Susan Hayden (2023)
Maze Mouth, Brian Sonia-Wallace (2023)
Tangled by Blood, Rebecca Evans (2023)
Another Way of Loving Death, Jeremy Ra (2023)
Kissing the Wound, J.D. Isip (2023)
Feed It to the River, Terhi K. Cherry (2022)
*Beat Not Beat: An Anthology of California Poets Screwing
    on the Beat and Post-Beat Tradition* (2022)
*When There Are Nine: Poems Celebrating the Life and Achievements
    of Ruth Bader Ginsburg* (2022)
The Knife Thrower's Daughter, Terri Niccum (2022)
2 Revere Place, Aruni Wijesinghe (2022)
Here Go the Knives, Kelsey Bryan-Zwick (2022)

Trumpets in the Sky, Jerry Garcia (2022)

Threnody, Donna Hilbert (2022)

A Burning Lake of Paper Suns, Ellen Webre (2021)

Instructions for an Animal Body, Kelly Gray (2021)

*Head *V* Heart: New & Selected Poems,* Rob Sturma (2021)

Sh!t Men Say to Me: A Poetry Anthology in Response to Toxic Masculinity (2021)

Flower Grand First, Gustavo Hernandez (2021)

Everything is Radiant Between the Hates, Rich Ferguson (2020)

When the Pain Starts: Poetry as Sequential Art, Alan Passman (2020)

This Place Could Be Haunted If I Didn't Believe in Love,
     Lincoln McElwee (2020)

Impossible Thirst, Kathryn de Lancellotti (2020)

Lullabies for End Times, Jennifer Bradpiece (2020)

Crabgrass World, Robin Axworthy (2020)

Contortionist Tongue, Dania Ayah Alkhouli (2020)

The only thing that makes sense is to grow, Scott Ferry (2020)

Dead Letter Box, Terri Niccum (2019)

Tea and Subtitles: Selected Poems 1999-2019, Michael Miller (2019)

At the Table of the Unknown, Alexandra Umlas (2019)

The Book of Rabbits, Vince Trimboli (2019)

Everything I Write Is a Love Song to the World, David McIntire (2019)

Letters to the Leader, HanaLena Fennel (2019)

Darwin's Garden, Lee Rossi (2019)

Dark Ink: A Poetry Anthology Inspired by Horror (2018)

Drop and Dazzle, Peggy Dobreer (2018)

Junkie Wife, Alexis Rhone Fancher (2018)

The Moon, My Lover, My Mother, & the Dog, Daniel McGinn (2018)

Lullaby of Teeth: An Anthology of Southern California Poetry (2017)

Angels in Seven, Michael Miller (2016)

A Likely Story, Robbi Nester (2014)

Embers on the Stairs, Ruth Bavetta (2014)

The Green of Sunset, John Brantingham (2013)

The Savagery of Bone, Timothy Matthew Perez (2013)

The Silence of Doorways, Sharon Venezio (2013)

Cosmos: An Anthology of Southern California Poetry (2012)

Straws and Shadows, Irena Praitis (2012)

In the Lake of Your Bones, Peggy Dobreer (2012)
I Was Building Up to Something, Susan Davis (2011)
Hopeless Cases, Michael Kramer (2011)
One World, Gail Newman (2011)
What We Ache For, Eric Morago (2010)
Now and Then, Lee Mallory (2009)
Pop Art: An Anthology of Southern California Poetry (2009)
In the Heaven of Never Before, Carine Topal (2008)
A Wild Region, Kate Buckley (2008)
Carving in Bone: An Anthology of Orange County Poetry (2007)
Kindness from a Dark God, Ben Trigg (2007)
A Thin Strand of Lights, Ricki Mandeville (2006)
Sleepyhead Assassins, Mindy Nettifee (2006)
Tide Pools: An Anthology of Orange County Poetry (2006)
Lost American Nights: Lyrics & Poems, Michael Ubaldini (2006)

Patrons

Moon Tide Press would like to thank the following people for their support in helping publish the finest poetry from the Southern California region. To sign up as a patron, visit www.moontidepress.com or send an email to publisher@moontidepress.com.

Anonymous
Robin Axworthy
Conner Brenner
Nicole Connolly
Bill Cushing
Susan Davis
Kristen Baum DeBeasi
Peggy Dobreer
Kate Gale
Dennis Gowans
Alexis Rhone Fancher
HanaLena Fennel
Half Off Books & Brad T. Cox
Donna Hilbert
Jim & Vicky Hoggatt
Michael Kramer
Ron Koertge & Bianca Richards
Gary Jacobelly
Ray & Christi Lacoste

Jeffery Lewis
Zachary & Tammy Locklin
Lincoln McElwee
David McIntire
José Enrique Medina
Michael Miller & Rachanee Srisavasdi
Michelle & Robert Miller
Ronny & Richard Morago
Terri Niccum
Andrew November
Jeremy Ra
Luke & Mia Salazar
Jennifer Smith
Roger Sponder
Andrew Turner
Rex Wilder
Mariano Zaro
Wes Bryan Zwick